W. Francis Gates

In Praise of Music

366 Selections - One for Every Day in the Year

W. Francis Gates

In Praise of Music
366 Selections - One for Every Day in the Year

ISBN/EAN: 9783744679428

Printed in Europe, USA, Canada, Australia, Japan

Cover: Foto ©Thomas Meinert / pixelio.de

More available books at **www.hansebooks.com**

IN PRAISE OF MUSIC

THREE HUNDRED AND SIXTY-SIX SELECTIONS

ONE FOR EVERY DAY IN THE YEAR

*FROM ANCIENT AND MODERN WRITERS
CONCERNING THE BEAUTIES AND BENEFITS OF
MUSIC AND MUSICAL STUDY*

EDITED BY W. FRANCIS GATES

PHILADELPHIA
THEODORE PRESSER
1898

DORNAN, PRINTER
PHILADELPHIA

TO

MY FRIEND

EDWARD BAXTER PERRY

LIST OF TITLES.

LIST OF TITLES.

(REFERENCED TO NUMBER OF THE SELECTION.)

1. Present or Future	*Richter.*
2. Music Helpful	*Ruskin.*
3. Fire from Man, Tears from Woman	*Beethoven.*
4. No Evil in Music	*Dewey.*
5.	*Plato.*
6.	*Beattie.*
7. To Upraise Mankind	*Perry.*
8. A Rhythmic Mind	*Beethoven.*
9. Music a Prayer	*Dwight.*
10. Church Song	*St. Augustine.*
11.	*Chateaubriand.*
12. The Shame of Degrading Music	*Abbott.*
13. Effective Music	*Zelter.*
14.	*Byrd.*
15. Searching Harmonies	*Eliot.*
16.	*Lanier.*
17. Hearing the Voice of the Dead	*Stainer.*
18. Self-Contemplation	*Ehlert.*
19.	*Johnson.*
20. The Summit	*Munger.*
21. The Power of Music upon the Uncultured	*Willeby.*
22.	*Finck.*
23.	*D'Israeli.*
24. Two Considerations	*Allen.*
25. Music and Government	*Confucius.*
26. The Universal Art	*Work.*

(v)

LIST OF TITLES.

27. Instrumental Music . . . . . *Hiller.*
28. . . . . *Holland.*
29. The Essence of Music . . . . *Thibaut.*
30. . . . . *Schopenhauer.*
31. Absolute Music . . . . . . *Ritter.*
32. Music and Poetry. . . . . . *Hugo.*
33. . . . . *D'Israeli.*
34. Melody . . . . *Haydn.*
35. The First Sound in Creation . . . *Upton.*
36. Praises for the Gift of Music . . . *Luther.*
37. . . . . *Schumann.*
38. Melody for Song . . . . . *Hoffmann.*
39. Education Without Music . . . . *Richter.*
40. Emotional Representation . . . . *Ritter.*
41. . . . . *Aristides.*
42. The Composer's Service to Art . . . *Pauer.*
43. A Heavenly Art . . . . . *Mendelssohn.*
44. . . . . *Shorthouse.*
45. The Extent of Music . . . . . *Hegel.*
46. Look Within . . . . . . *Benbow.*
47. The Purest of Arts . . . . . *Wagner.*
48. Devotional Music . . . . . *Mason.*
49. From Slight Material . . . . *Chadwick.*
50. For All . . . . *Ritter.*
51. Marvels from Sound . . . . . *Church.*
52. Phases of Composition . . . . *Upton.*
53. . . . . *Carlyle.*
54. . . . . *Beethoven.*
55. From Heaven Rather than Earth . . *Praetorius.*
56. Programme Music . . . . . *Perry.*
57. . . . . *Upton.*
58. Many-Sided Music . . . . . *Van Cleve.*
59. . . . . *De Staël.*
60. Art for the Poor . . . . . *Damrosch.*
61. Incentive to Piety . . . . . *Weber.*
62. . . . . *Ruskin.*

63. Music as Pleasure	*Gates.*
64. No Dearth of Literature	*Van Cleve.*
65. Intellect plus Emotion	*Fillmore.*
66. Supernal Beauty	*Poe.*
67. The All-Sufficiency of Music	*Emerson.*
68. . . , ...	*Haydn.*
69.	*Finck.*
70. Sweet Pleasure	*Doerner.*
71. To Every Mood	*Prentice.*
72. Beyond	*Shorthouse.*
73. The Highest Reason for Musical Study	*Parry.*
74. Music in the Air	*Luther.*
75. Three Elements	*Niecks.*
76.	*Waller.*
77. Extension of Musical Knowledge	*Anon.*
78. Beauty	*Henry.*
79. Room for Improvement	*Anon.*
80. A Glorious Gift	*Praetorius.*
81. Cheerfulness	*Euripides.*
82. Music Suggestive	*Sherwood.*
83. Song Universal	*Anon.*
84. Perfection	*Whiting.*
85. A Soul Gymnastic	*Ruskin.*
86. Music Moves the Heart	*Gladden.*
87. As an Educator	*Anon.*
88. A Strange Bird	*Holland.*
89. Music and Love	*Weber.*
90.	*Spencer.*
91. Music a Necessity of Nature	*Sullivan.*
92. In Mysterious Tones	*Hoffmann.*
93. Permanency of the Best	*Ruskin.*
94. A Product of the Imagination	*Henry.*
95. A Rule of Life	*Goodrich.*
96. Pleasure in Art	*Hiller.*
97. Our Reasons for Singing	*Ruskin.*
98.	*Hueffer.*

99. Subtle Music	. . . . .	*Eastlake.*
100.	. . . . . .	*Beethoven.*
101. Antiquity of Music	. . . .	*Trotter.*
102. For Love, Not Command	. . .	*Rubinstein.*
103. To Soothe and Soften	. . .	*White.*
104. Cultivated Enjoyment	. . .	*Hiller.*
105. Music Cultivates our Better Natures	. .	*Perry.*
106. In the Heart of Man	. . . .	*Hoffmann.*
107. The Divine Organist	. . .	*Ruskin.*
108. Realism	. . . . .	*Anon.*
109.	. . . . . .	*Plato.*
110. Intellect Subordinate to Emotion	. .	*Ayres.*
111. Songless Women	. . . .	*Anderson.*
112. These not from Music	. . .	*Avison.*
113.	. . . . . .	*Mirandola.*
114. Joy, not Sadness	. . . .	*Abbott.*
115. Superior Emotional Endowment	. .	*Perry.*
116.	. . . . . .	*Bevan.*
117. Music as Mediator	. . . .	*Beethoven.*
118.	. . . . . .	*Addison.*
119. Music is Revealed Beauty	. . .	*Henry.*
120. Vitality Through Music	. . .	*Apthorp.*
121.	. . . . . .	*Schumann.*
122. Great Art from Great Nations	. .	*Benbow.*
123.	. . . . . .	*Hiller.*
124. Music is Real	. . . . .	*Chadwick.*
125. Intellectual *vs.* Emotional Music	. .	*Elson.*
126. Its Elevating Power	. . . .	*Perry.*
127. As no Other Can Do	. . .	*Upton.*
128. Both Specialize and Generalize	. .	*Van Cleve.*
129. The Influence of Music	. . .	*Merz.*
130. A Reliable Guide	. . . .	*Ritter.*
131.	. . . . . .	*Auerbach.*
132. A Mental Stimulus	. . . .	*Gates.*
133. Begin in Childhood	. . . .	*Henry.*
134. Ignorance Should Humiliate	. .	*Krehbiel.*

LIST OF TITLES.

135.	Emotional Discipline	*Haweis.*
136.	The Most Effectual Art	*Halle.*
137.	Not very Dangerous to Morals	*Addison.*
138.	The Nature of Music	*Fetis.*
139.	Music Develops Character	*Anon.*
140.	.	*Anon.*
141.	Exceeded Only by Metaphysics	*Merz.*
142.	.	*Shorthouse.*
143.	The Arts Compared	*Church.*
144.	.	*Lytton.*
145.	Music a Healer	*Haweis.*
146.	Not to be Defined	*Lully.*
147.	A Serious Matter	*Mendelssohn.*
148.	Music the Nurse of the Soul	*Bertini.*
149.	From the Cradle to the Grave	*Abbott.*
150.	Virtue in Music	*Luther.*
151.	Music Criticism	*Bach.*
152.	Music and Love	*Hiller.*
153.	It Refines and Soothes	*Hall.*
154.	A Voice from the Eighteenth Century	*Burney.*
155.	Music's Refining Power	*Lytton.*
156.	A Universal Language	*Lombard.*
157.	.	*Longfellow.*
158.	A Voice from the Sixteenth Century	*Hooker.*
159.	Unity in Variety	*Liszt.*
160.	Praise for the Piano	*Haweis.*
161.	Its Spirit is Love	*Wagner.*
162.	The Minor Key	*Anon.*
163.	An Ideal Representation	*Carriere.*
164.	Music in the Home	*Landon.*
165.	Refine the Taste	*Prentice.*
166.	.	*Luther.*
167.	Sentiment and Science	*Berlioz.*
168.	.	*Montesquieu.*
169.	Music Extending its Sway	*Anon.*
170.	Each His Own Measure	*Schopenhauer.*

171. All Deep Things are Song	. . .	Carlyle.
172. God's Best Gift	. . . .	Landon.
173.	. . . . . .	Wagner.
174. The Heart the Interpreter	. . .	Goodrich.
175. True of the Enthusiast	. . .	Anon.
176. Morals	. . . . .	Bryant.
177. A Common Origin	. . . .	Ritter.
178. Not Second to Intellect	. . .	Spencer.
179. A Poetical Medium of Expression	. .	Macfarran.
180. A Classic View	. . . .	Plato.
181. Solace in Music	. . . .	Lytton.
182. Echoes from Above	. . . .	Anon.
183.	. . . . . .	Ayres.
184. The Beginnings of Music	. . .	Gates.
185. To Discipline Emotion	. . .	Haweis.
186.	. . . . . .	Schumann.
187. How Many Realize It?	. . .	Anon.
188. To the Heart	. . . . .	Merz.
189. A Natural Means of Expression	. .	Sill.
190. Music in Speech	. . . .	Carlyle.
191. Farther than Speech	. . . .	Dwight.
192. Added Force	. . . . .	Bellars.
193. Art Growth	. . . . .	Liszt.
194. Teach Your Children Music	. .	Walpole.
195. Highly Specialized Art	. . .	Mathews.
196. Rhythm and Beauty	. . . .	Christiani.
197. The View of a Lawmaker	. . .	Bonaparte.
198. The Art of the Prophets	. . .	Luther.
199.	. . . . . .	Homer.
200. Music Makes Character	. . .	Goldbeck.
201. A Means of Culture	. . . .	Merz.
202.	. . . . . .	Haweis.
203. The Object of Music	. . . .	Schumann.
204. With Sweet Emotion	. . . .	Bach.
205. The Musical Brain	. . . .	Holmes.
206. A Natural Medium	. . . .	Austin.

LIST OF TITLES.

207. The Pure Art . . . . . . *Abbott.*
208. Not to be Contaminated . . . . *Moffat.*
209. Mistress of Order . . . . . *Luther.*
210. A Memory Cultivation . . . . *Gates.*
211. Upon Our Heart Strings . . . . *Merz.*
212. An Inclusive View . . . . . *Bartlett.*
213. A Divine Calling . . . . . *Mendelssohn.*
214. A Woman's View . . . . . *Ouida.*
215. Sound Expresses Feeling; Words, Ideas . *Fillmore.*
216. In Spite of Abuse . . . . . *Hiller.*
217. Incompatible Traits . . . . . *Dawson.*
218. Awakening the Better Nature . . . *Damrosch.*
219. Straight to the Heart . . . . *Kingsley.*
220.   . . . . *Giles.*
221. Music Covers the Whole Emotional Gamut *Chambers.*
222. A Novelist's Musical Nature . . . *Daudet.*
223. For the Masses . . . . . *Merz.*
224. Grand Music . . . . . . *Haughton.*
225. An Element of Culture . . . . *Dwight.*
226. A Plea for Early Cultivation . . . *Powers.*
227. The Greatest Art . . . . . *Dawson.*
228. Concrete and Abstract Musicians . . *Klauser.*
229. Better Some Music than No Music . . *Kohler.*
230.   . . . . *Gurney.*
231. Echoes from Heaven . . . . *Newman.*
232. A Notable Saying . . . . . *Goethe.*
233. Do Something Worthy . . . . *Longfellow.*
234. Communicated Feeling . . . . *Ritter.*
235. A Concise Definition . . . . *Berlioz.*
236.   . . . . *Leibnitz.*
237. Gladstone's Views . . . . . *Gladstone.*
238. Its Purpose . . . . . . *Hooker.*
239. Finer than Speech . . . . . *Dwight.*
240. A Partial Knowledge . . . . *Richter.*
241. Crystallized Sound . . . . . *Thoreau.*
242.   . . . . *Anon.*

LIST OF TITLES.

243. Preaches Universal Brotherhood . . *Dickinson.*
244. . . . . *Weber.*
245. Modern as an Art . . . . *Anon.*
246. A Poetic Fancy . . . . *Richter.*
247. Theory as a Foundation . . . *Anon.*
248. What Music Requires of Us. . . *Gates.*
249. There are also Weeds . . . *Christiani.*
250. The Outcome of Character . . *Hadow.*
251. At Lowest Ebb . . . . *Borst.*
252. . . . . *Wordsworth.*
253. The Essence of Music . . . *Krüger.*
254. Music not the Cause of Failure . *Smith.*
255. A Part of our Existence . . . *Stainer.*
256. A Statesman and Warrior . . *Bismarck.*
257. . . . . *Anon.*
258. Sense, Intellect, and Emotion . . *Dickinson.*
259. Rhythmic Architecture . . . *Hegel.*
260. To Make Men Content . . . *Anon.*
261. Pure Art . . . . . . *Bellars.*
262. Recreation for Mind and Body . . *Beveridge.*
263. An Inherent Power . . . . *Franz.*
264. The Speech of Angels . . . *Carlyle.*
265. Music's Uses . . . . . *Chomet.*
266. A Narrower View . . . . *Berlioz.*
267. Creation's Harmonies . . . *Mazzini.*
268. To Young People . . . . *Ruskin.*
269. What Music in Heaven? . . . *Walton.*
270. . . . . *Praetorius.*
271. Music Never Corrupt . . . *Abbott.*
272. Music Should be Pleasing . . *Mozart.*
273. . . . . *Ovid.*
274. Music is Suggestive . . . . *Anon.*
275. Superiority of Vocal Music . . *Bunsen.*
276. Music is Non-Material . . . *Goethe.*
277. Seek Good Music, not Bad . . *Smith.*
278. . . . . *Wagner.*

279. Familiarity Breeds Greater Delight	. .	*Goethe.*
280. Music Associated with Sense Perception	.	*Hegel.*
281. Music in the Public Schools	. . .	*Hawley.*
282. Who, Then, Gets to the End?	. . .	*Schumann.*
283.	. . . .	*Schumann.*
284. The Expression of the Immaterial	. .	*Haweis.*
285. Music's Refining Tone	. . . .	*Gluck.*
286.	. . . .	*Hanslick.*
287. The Joyous Art	. . . . .	*Dickinson.*
288. Inarticulate Speech	. . . . .	*Carlyle.*
289. No Sweeter Voice	. . . . .	*Burritt.*
290. Is Music Aristocratic?	. . . .	*Anon.*
291. Abstract Training	. . . . .	*Anon.*
292. The Governor of the Heart	. . .	*Luther.*
293. Effective Music	. . . . .	*Thibaut.*
294. Materia Musica	. . . . .	*Helmholtz.*
295. Genius in Music	. . . . .	*Schumann.*
296.	. . . .	*Ambros.*
297. Music the Language of the Emotions	.	*Haweis.*
298. Threefold Benefit	. . . . .	*Schumann.*
299. Music not a Trifle	. . . . .	*Gladstone.*
300. Folk Music of Antiquity	. . . .	*Thomas.*
301. Live In It	, ...	*Franz.*
302. The Voice the Living Instrument	. .	*Marx.*
303. Artistic Ramifications	. . . .	*Tapper.*
304. The Eternity of Music	. . . .	*Upton.*
305.	. . . .	*Milton.*
306. An Intense Pleasure	. . . ` . .	*Schumann.*
307. A Philosopher's Musings	. . . .	*Mill.*
308. No Corrupt Music	. . . . .	*Burney.*
309. An Unpleasant Truth	. . . .	*Ritter.*
310.	. . . .	*Tapper.*
311. Our Music is a Modern Art	. . .	*Berlioz.*
312. Music Needed in America	. . .	*Finck.*
313. Study Music as Literature	. . .	*Mathews.*
314. Music is Independent	. . . .	*Fetis.*

315. No Denominationalism in Music	*Abbott.*
316. The Misuse of Music	*Morales.*
317. A Beautiful Expression	*Goethe.*
318. Words Do not Explain Music	*Mendelssohn.*
319. Always Appropriate	*Trotter.*
320. Life is Music	*Ruskin.*
321. The Power of Indefiniteness	*Lombard.*
322. The Divinity of Music	*Thibaut.*
323. Musical Study Productive of True Culture	*Gates.*
324. Music the Gift of God	*Thibaut.*
325. Earthly Grammar of Heaven's Language	*Hanna.*
326. A Foretaste of Another World	*Landon.*
327. Full of Truth and Beauty	*Tapper.*
328.	*Gurney.*
329. Singing Praises with the Understanding	*Fuller.*
330. Art only to Those who Appreciate it	*Anon.*
331. Happy People	*Smith.*
332. The Power of Music	*Drury.*
333. Woman's Song	*Upton.*
334. All Phases of Passion	*Sinclair.*
335. The Mission of the Musician	*Jeffers.*
336. Quickening the Mind	*Hill.*
337.	*Richter.*
338. Full of Religion	*Upton.*
339. Music in the Service of Religion	*Ella.*
340. Music in Child Education	*Wakefield.*
341. Conditioned on Love	*Krehbiel.*
342. Music Humanizing and Social	*Ritter.*
343.	*Edwards.*
344. Musical Genius	*Crowest.*
345. The Lasting Pleasure of Music	*Ella.*
346. Music Next to Theology	*Luther.*
347. Music the Breath of Germany	*Hugo.*
348. Music a Reflection of its Epoch	*Rubinstein.*
349. Abstract Emotions	*Henderson.*
350. The Dual Nature of Music	*Krehbiel.*

LIST OF TITLES.

351.	. . . .	*Cicero.*
352.	Exterior Influences Affect Music .	*Skinner.*
353.	To Refine our Taste	*Prentice.*
354.	No Melody, No Music . . .	*Christiani.*
355.	Sentiment *vs.* Sentimentalism . .	*Merz.*
356.	The Basis of Musical Power . .	*Allen.*
357.	Incompetent Judges	*Ritter.*
358.	History in Music	*Tapper.*
359.	A Musical Fancy	*Hazlitt.*
360.	Fanatics and Devils	*Mower.*
361.	A Modern Art	*Schumann.*
362.	Music and Other Arts . . .	*Hadow.*
363.	Music an Intellectual Product . .	*Henderson.*
364.	Eternal, Not Temporal . . .	*Wagner.*
365.	Its Ultimate Mission . . .	*Spencer.*
366.	A Long and Glorious Record . .	*Parry.*

IN PRAISE OF MUSIC.

IN PRAISE OF MUSIC.

1.
Present or Future?   Jan. 1st.

O music, thou who bringest the receding waves of eternity nearer to the weary heart of man, as he stands upon the shore and longs to cross over, art thou the evening breeze of this life, or the morning air of the future?   JEAN PAUL RICHTER.

2.
Music Helpful.   Jan. 2d.

Music is the nearest at hand, the most orderly, the most delicate, and the most perfect of all bodily pleasures; it is also the only one which is equally helpful to all the ages of man—helpful from the nurse's song to her infant, to the music, unheard of others, which often, if not most frequently, haunts the deathbed of pure and innocent spirits.   RUSKIN.

3.
Fire from Man, Tears from Woman.   Jan. 3d.

Music should strike fire from the heart of man and bring tears from the eyes of woman.
    BEETHOVEN.

4.
Jan. 4th.   **No Evil in Music.**

No chord of music ever touched any evil passion. I have heard of, but never listened to, any music that could, with propriety, be called voluptuous. Words wedded to music often are, but melody—*never*. All sweet sounds bear the soul up into the world of pure moral feeling and sense; hence, music is the noblest minister to religion. I would have music *well* taught in every family, as I would establish the family altar.

DR. DEWEY.

Jan. 5th.   5.

Love teacheth music. PLATO.

Jan. 6th.   6.

Is there a heart that music cannot melt?
BEATTIE.

7.
Jan. 7th.   **To Upraise Mankind.**

Music, the most versatile of the arts, consequently the most varied and exhaustless in the æsthetic pleasure which it affords, is a potent lever, when properly employed, for the upraising of mankind. That every musician is not the highest type of man proves merely that the most powerful lever cannot always raise poor humanity to the level of the angels and sustain it at that elevation for an entire lifetime. But even a temporary ascent into higher, purer regions is certainly better than grovelling in the dust altogether, as would be the case with such men otherwise. Who decries religion because every professor is not a saint, or poetry because every poet has not always lived up to his ideals? No one can claim that the most faithless disciple would have been better without any religion at all; and none dare say that without his music the most unworthy musician and his thousands of listeners would not have been worse or that without poetry the poet and the world would have been better.

The mission of art and the artist is to crystallize and present to us, in enduring and attractive forms, the best in human experience. We should regard music precisely as we do the other arts, reasonably, yet reverently, neither as an incomprehensible emanation from Divinity, nor as a frivolous pleasure and pastime, but as one of the purest and most potent, though always human, agents for human gratification, elevation, and development. EDW. BAXTER PERRY.

8.
A Rhythmic Mind. Jan. 8th.

Music alone ushers man into the portal of an intellectual world, ready to encompass him, but which he may never encompass. That mind alone whose every thought is rhythm can embody music, can comprehend its mysteries, its divine inspirations, and can alone speak to the senses of its intellectual revelations.
BEETHOVEN.

9.
Music a Prayer. Jan. 9th.

Every genuine strain of music is a serene prayer, or bold inspired demand, to be united with all at the heart of all things. DWIGHT.

10.
Church Song. Jan. 10th.

How abundantly did I weep before God, to hear those hymns of thine; being touched to the very quick by the voices of thy sweet church song. The voices flowed into my ears, which caused the affections of my devotion to overflow, and my tears to run over; and happy did I find myself therein. SAINT AUGUSTINE.

Jan. 11th.   11.

Music is the child of prayer, the companion of religion. CHATEAUBRIAND.

12.

Jan. 12th.   **The Shame of Degrading Music.**

Music comes into our world as sunlight streams into a room. It may be full of motes, but the sunlight is still pure, despite the motes. We may, out of our evil imaginations, out of our base thoughts, fill the pure strains of music that float in the air with motes—aye! with grosser particles—but the music is still independent of them. The voice of music is the voice of the three purest creatures God has made—birds, children, and angels. Oh, the shame of degrading music! Oh, the shame of degrading that which God made to be the medium by which the angels should tell the world that a Redeemer had come! Oh, the shame of so mating it to words as to fire sensual passions and stir the mind to evil thinking! Oh, the dishonor of making music a vehicle of cant and hypocrisy, the utterance of prayer when there is no praying, the expression of reverence when there is no reverence, the expression of love when the heart beats with no love! "Thou shalt not take the name of the Lord thy God in vain." I sometimes think there is no place where that commandment is so often violated as in the church; sometimes by ministers uttering prayers when there is no prayer in their hearts; sometimes by choirs singing words of praise when there is no praise in their hearts. LYMAN ABBOTT.

13.
Effective Music. Jan. 13th.

Just as the writer who speaks to the heart is sure to please, so is a composer who gives the player something which he can play and enjoy himself, and make others enjoy too. ZELTER.

14. Jan. 14th.

Music loosens a heart that care has bound.
BYRD.

15.
Searching Harmonies. Jan. 15th.

Is it any weakness, pray, to be wrought on by exquisite music? To feel its wondrous harmonies searching the subtlest windings of your soul, the delicate fibres of life where no memory can penetrate, and binding together your whole being, past and present, in one unspeakable vibration, melting you in one moment with all the tenderness, all the love that has been scattered through the toilsome years, concentrating in one emotion of heroic courage or resignation all the hard-learned lessons of self-renouncing sympathy, blending your present joy with past sorrow, and your present sorrow with all your past joy. GEORGE ELIOT.

16. Jan. 16th.

Music is love in search of a word.
SIDNEY LANIER.

17.

Jan. 17th.   **Hearing the Voice of the Dead.**

Modern music has brought under observation, perhaps into existence, a group of phenomena, mental and physical, which we know and feel to be, and which have already set in motion a widespread desire for analysis, description, and classification. To live in happy ignorance of these occult phenomena of music is to walk along the path of life unaware of one of the most strange and fascinating outbursts of mental activity which this century has seen. We have gradually been brought face to face with the fact that the succession, combination, color, and contrast of sounds can provide a genius with the means of depicting his emotional state, can embody the very outpouring of his soul; and, what is more remarkable, that sympathetic listeners, in so far as they possess a share of the composer's temperament and have had the necessary training, can not only interpret his expressions, they do actually have the same feelings and drift into the same emotional condition which guided his pen as he wrote. When we listen to a symphony by Beethoven we are no longer merely trying to drive away for a time the care and worry of daily routine in a pleasant and harmless amusement, we are engaged in something far higher, far more searching, far more touching than that, we are hearing the voice of one who is dead, telling us in no uncertain language the story of some phase of his innermost life on earth. The narration may be almost unconsciously made, but this shows it to be absolutely truthful, and renders it doubly incisive.
                                              JOHN STAINER.

18.
Self-Contemplation.   Jan. 18th.

Music is the contemplation of ourselves, our purest and best qualities. She is the mysterious power that subdues our sorrows and satisfies our joys. Her ever-present consoling influence fortifies our souls with almost all the force possessed by religion, and I doubt if the charm, with which she raises us out of ourselves, can find a parallel in the kingdom of magic.

LOUIS EHLERT.

19.   Jan. 19th.

Music is the only sensual pleasure without vice.

SAMUEL JOHNSON.

20.
The Summit.   Jan. 20th.

Emotion is the summit of existence, and music is the summit of emotion, the art pathway to God.

J. J. MUNGER.

21.
Power of Music Upon the Uncultured.   Jan. 21st.

Music is not mere pastime. Its effects are both powerful and beneficial, not only upon the cultured few, but upon the uncultured many. Says the Rev. Dr. Haweis: " I have known the oratorio of the ' Messiah' draw the lowest dregs of Whitechapel into a church to hear it, and during the performance sobs have broken forth from the silent and attentive throng. Will any one say that for these people to have their feelings for once put through such a noble and long-sustained exercise as that could be otherwise than beneficial?"

If the lower orders could have as much of music as

of the low literature with which they beguile their spare hours, there would be a large decrease in crime. Music imparts only good influences, while this low class of literature incites its votaries to commit the crimes and practice the vices of which they read. Music could be made the means to wean the people from the low pleasures which brutalize and debase.

CHARLES WILLEBY.

Jan. 22d.   22.

One of the most important functions of music is that of weaning the people from low and demoralizing pleasures. HENRY T. FINCK.

Jan. 23d.   23.

Music is a stimulant to mental exertion.
D'ISRAELI.

24.
Jan. 24th.   **Two Considerations.**

As bearing upon the compatibility of attention to music and devotion to what is commonly considered the more serious business of manhood, we have a strong argument in the career of the reformer Luther, the soldiers Frederick the Great and von Moltke, not to speak of the present Emperor of Germany, or of our own politician, Carl Schurz. Among poets might be mentioned Shakespeare, Milton, Goethe, Moore, Browning, and Lanier as pre-eminent in the union of poetical power with extraordinary knowledge of music.

Whilst poetry, painting, and sculpture, as independent arts, are susceptible of debasing influences, music is always elevating. If it ever appears otherwise, it is through association with such arts as have inherent capability of ministering to immorality.

Music is the one art pertaining to our existence here which has promise of immortality in the next life. As long as there is a call for loving, trusting, and obeying our Maker, so long will there be a call for praising him with all the resources of our divine art. Ideal manhood culminates in such service, and whatever ministers to this end cannot be overestimated.

B. D. ALLEN.

25.
Music and Government.   Jan. 25th.

Wouldst thou know if a people be well governed, if its laws be good or bad? examine the music it practises.

CONFUCIUS.

26.
The Universal Art.   Jan. 26th.

It can be said with absolute truth that there is no soul in all the realm of creation that is not susceptible to music. It is the one power that seems to have an unfailing charm for the universal soul. The truer the name, therefore, which it has won—" the divine art." Surely it is suggestive of the " divinity that stirs within us," when we find all souls open widely or less wide to one strong passion, one upward-tending affection, one all-subduing emotion. Sweet and beautiful the Providence that has left in our sin-begirt humanity the capacity to feel the tenderness and the majesty of this power. Sufficient proof this that God never intended to give this world over to a reprobate condition, when he left among us such mighty counter-agents of sin and unholiness.

The Germans even say that bad people do not have songs—such is the confidence of one nation in the heaven-born origin and influence of the art.

What comforts the soul is the belief that there lives a great tone master, a powerful director, who will work out through many discords, and many disenchantments, and many breakings of separate instruments, an ultimate divine harmony. All music of the individual soul should help to this end. Let each do his duty in the great chorus, performing well his part, and the harmony comes. E. W. WORK.

27.
Jan. 27th. **Instrumental Music.**

Strictly instrumental music, such as our great masters have bequeathed to us in their symphonies, quartettes, and sonatas, is, perhaps, the only artistic production in which the Germans stand alone, not only without legitimate, but really without rivals. But there is no branch of the art which, in order to be correctly and completely understood, demands from the listener greater attention and devotion. F. HILLER.

Jan. 28th. 28.

Music is a strange bird singing the songs of another shore. J. G. HOLLAND.

29.
Jan. 29th. **The Essence of Music.**

No art is without a living principle; and this may be easily found in music, by going back to the point where it took its rise and became a want. In other words, music is, in its essence, nothing but, as it were, the overflowing of emotion — of mental ecstasy — in sound; and whenever a piece of music answers to this description it will never fail to move and enchant all unprejudiced minds, barring, of course, that exceptional class that have no sense of tune, and to whom music is a sealed book, like a statue to a blind man.

THIBAUT.

30.   Jan. 30th.

Music is as a shower-bath of the soul, washing away all that is impure.   SCHOPENHAUER.

31.
Absolute Music.   Jan. 31st.

Absolute music has only the power to express emotions of the soul, humor, sensations, whether called forth by inner or outward impressions. Of all the arts it does it most emphatically and conclusively, but also, at the same time, most undecidedly; that is, inasmuch as the life of motion, from which it emanates, cannot act in common like the life of intellect. If there is less misunderstanding possible in the life of the intellect, in the comprehending of thoughts by a logical development of ideas, then the musical powers of expression which do not emanate from the understanding, the intellect, but emanate from the inner intuition, are open to many misunderstandings. If music by its power acts ever so convincingly, there is still required a certain acquiescence, a good faith in music and its power of expression, in the respective listener, as well as a certain accordance of his life of emotion with that of the tone-poet, so as to arrive at a complete enjoyment.

HERMANN RITTER.

32.
Feb. 1st.   **Music and Poetry.**

Music is the vapor of art. It is to poetry what reverie is to thought, what fluid is to liquid, what the ocean of clouds is to the ocean of waves.

Victor Hugo.

Feb. 2d.   33.

Were it not for music we might in these days say the beautiful is dead.   D'Israeli.

34.
Feb. 3d.   **Melody.**

It is the melody which is the charm of music; it is also that which is the most difficult to produce. The invention of a fine melody is a work of genius. The truth is, a fine melody needs neither ornaments nor accessories to please. Would you know whether it be really fine? Strip it of its accompaniments.

Haydn.

35.
Feb. 4th.   **The First Sound in Creation.**

Music was the first sound heard in the creation, when the morning stars sang together. It was the first sound heard at the birth of Christ, when the angels sang together above the plains of Bethlehem. It is the universal language, which appeals to the universal heart of mankind. It greets our entrance into this world, and solemnizes our departure. Its thrill pervades all Nature —in the hum of the tiniest insect, in the tops of the wind-smitten pines, in the solemn diapason of the ocean.

And there must come a time when it will be the only suggestion left of our human nature and the creation, since it alone, of all things on earth, is known in heaven. The human soul and music are alone eternal.

GEORGE P. UPTON.

36.
Praises for the Gift of Music.   Feb. 5th.

I wished from my heart to praise and extol that beautiful and artistical gift of God, the liberal art of music; but I find that it is of such great utility and is such a noble and majestic art, that I do not know where I should begin or end praising it, or in what manner and form I should praise it, as indeed it meriteth praise and the love and esteem of every one, and I am hence so much overpowered by the rich fulness of the praise of this art, that I cannot extol it sufficiently, for who can say and show all that might be written and spoken on this subject? Yea, even if one would say and show all, he would nevertheless forget much, and it is utterly impossible that this noble art can be praised enough.

MARTIN LUTHER.

37.   Feb. 6th.

Music is the expression of a refined nature.

SCHUMANN.

38.
Melody for Song.   Feb. 7th.

It is melody that is first and foremost in music, and affects human feelings with marvellous and magic power. It cannot be repeated too often that, without expressive melody, every ornament added by instrumentation is nothing but tawdry magnificence. The best definition of true melody, in a higher sense, is something that may be sung. Melody should be song itself, and as such should flow freely and spontaneously from the human heart. Melody which cannot be sung in that way is nothing more than a succession of individual sounds which strive in vain to become music. HOFFMAN.

39.
Feb. 8th. **Education Without Music.**

We cannot imagine a complete education of man without music. It is the gymnastic of the affections. In suitable connection with exercises, it is necessary to keep body and soul in health.
JEAN PAUL RICHTER.

40.
Feb. 9th. **Emotional Representation.**

To represent emotions of the soul can be done most profoundly in music. True, to a certain degree words can do it too; yet words can really only picture emotion of the soul by comparisons. To create an emotion of the soul in another person and thereby place the same in a position to live through it, just as I have felt it, is undoubtedly most intelligently and most markedly done by music. HERMANN RITTER.

Feb. 10th. 41.

Music is calculated to compose the mind and fit it for instruction. ARISTIDES.

42.
Feb. 11th. **The Composer's Service to Art.**

Music has become so popular, it has obtained such undisputed supremacy as a means of amusement and enjoyment, and sometimes of education and refinement, that we often forget to consider whence comes its surprising effect, its irresistible strength. Thousands of people rush to concerts and to operas, are delighted with the sweet sounds, the rich harmonies, the enchanting melodies which salute their ears; yet not one in each thousand will take the trouble to analyze the source of his enjoyment; and many, even if they endeavored to do so, would be unable to account for it.

In musical art nothing is left to mere chance. The composer has not only to learn all the hundreds of rules which regulate the prosaic part of his work, but he has to study nature; he must dive into the psychological mysteries of the human heart, must identify himself with the feeling which his subject demands; in short, the composer has to pass many an anxious hour before he can lay down his pen with the consciousness that he has faithfully served his art, that he has made good use of the talent which a Divine Power has entrusted to his care. ERNST PAUER.

43.
A Heavenly Art. Feb. 12th.

I now feel more vividly than ever what a heavenly calling art is, and for this also I have to thank my parents. Just when all else which ought to interest the mind appears repugnant and empty and insipid, the smallest real service to art lays hold of your inmost thoughts, leading you far away from town and country, and from earth itself; then it is indeed a blessing sent by God. MENDELSSOHN.

44. Feb. 13th.

In music all hearts are revealed to us.
SHORTHOUSE.

45.
Feb. 14th. **The Extent of Music.**

Music extends itself in every direction for the expression of all distinct sensations and shades of joyousness, serenity, humor, shoutings, and rejoicings of soul; as well as the graduations of anguish, sorrow, grief, lamentation, distress, pain, regret; and, finally, aspiration, worship, love, etc., belong to the proper sphere of musical expression. HEGEL.

46.
Feb. 15th. **Look Within.**

Our musical art affects us in two ways. It makes us more deeply and intimately acquainted with our own individual feelings, thus intensifying the Ego; and it puts us in touch with that common feeling that makes the whole world kin. It says to every man as an individual entity, "Know thyself—look within;" to man as part of the universal whole, "Love the world, its Maker, and its creatures."

There is also testimony of a negative character to help us appreciate the necessity of music. Taken as the handmaiden of religion, contrast its influence in the Puritan, modern Greek, and Jewish churches with other churches.

On all sides there is cumulative evidence that people are beginning to discover what music earnestly signifies.

It is shown by non-professional authorities that it is a matter of practical everyday import. It is for the mass of men, and not for the leisurely few only.

WM. BENBOW.

47.
The Purest of Arts.   Feb. 16th.

Whatever the relations of music, it will never cease to be the noblest and purest of arts. It is in the nature of music to bring before us, with absolute truth and reality, what other arts can only imply. Its inherent solemnity makes it so chaste and wonderful that it ennobles whatever comes in contact with it. WAGNER.

48.
Devotional Music.   Feb. 17th.

Music can move or melt an audience, and ought therefore to be made a powerful auxiliary to the faithful preacher. LOWELL MASON.

49.
From Slight Material.   Feb. 18th.

Every musical composition (if it be worthy of the name) is an art problem in which, with certain conditions given and certain materials at hand, a certain result is to be obtained. Its perfection as a result depends on the effective adaptation of the means to the end—its unity of form and contents—the appropriate relation of its outside and inside. This is equally true of any other work of art, whether it be a painting, or a poem, or a pile of buildings. The painter with a burnt match and the paper his luncheon is wrapped in, gives you a man who breathes; the architect with a few laths, some plaster, and a swamp gives you what Aladdin saw when he put the high light on his lamp; and Beethoven with four notes gives us the fifth symphony. GEO. W. CHADWICK.

50.

Feb. 19th.   **For All.**

Music is not individual property, but a gift for all. To every one a spring of purest and most refined education.
H. RITTER.

51.

Feb. 20th.   **Marvels From Sound.**

When we thoughtfully consider all that our art contains, the mind dwells on this record of the past that is our inheritance, to enrich it by the present, if we may, and to reverence and cherish it as a legacy of priceless value. What marvels the musical genius of the world has wrought from an invisible substance like sound! The painter or sculptor readily finds many scenes that may be transformed into pictures or statuary, reproduction, idealization, and the embodiment of some beautiful idea being all that they strive for. The musician, however, having nothing tangible before him, must yet create, like the devotees of other arts, a work from out a mass of sound that shall have complete form, and then, like Pygmalion of old, behold it come to life under his hand, and possess a living soul that will speak to us when we are lonely, and comfort us when we are sad; now leading us forth into the wide, wide world, and again remaining with us as companions of our solitude.

Bach, Handel, Haydn, Mozart, Beethoven, Schubert, Schumann, Mendelssohn, Weber, Glück, and Wagner; *they* are *our* sculptors, who have, like Michael Angelo, found the "angel" in the marble of sound.
L. R. CHURCH.

52.
Phases of Composition. Feb. 21st.

Beethoven has shown the depth of music, its majesty, its immortality; Mendelssohn its elegance of form; Handel its solemnity and grandeur; Mozart its wondrous grace and sweetness; Haydn its purity, freshness, and simplicity; Schumann its romance; Chopin its poetry and tender melancholy; Schubert its richness of melody; Bach its massive foundations; Berlioz its grotesqueness and supernaturalism; Liszt and Wagner its poetical idealism. UPTON.

53. Feb. 22d.

There is something deep and good in melody, for body and soul go strangely together. CARLYLE.

54. Feb. 23d.

Music herself teaches us harmony. BEETHOVEN.

55.
From Heaven Rather than Earth. Feb. 24th.

Music, in the opinion of many, ranks second only to faith and religion; and apart from its power, its effect, and its many advantages, we may justly regard it as belonging to heaven rather than to earth, awakening and stimulating, as it does, in our hearts a desire to praise the Almighty with psalms and thanksgivings.

MICHAEL PRAETORIUS.

56.
Programme Music. Feb. 25th.

Music, though unquestionably the vaguest and most ethereal of all the arts—the least of the earth, earthy—offers, nevertheless, an extensive field in which such episodes of life as by their nature are fitted for art treatment in any form, if embodied with taste and scholarship, may take an honorable and legitimate position—that known as programme music.

In listening to a composition of purely lyric character, it is the love of beauty inherent in the soul, it is the subtler, more ideal emotions latent in the heart, which are reached through the sense of hearing; in the noble representative of descriptive music, the intellect and the imagination are excited in addition, and the effect, if we grant it less potent in one direction, is widened, enriched, diversified. It is therefore restricting the power and scope of music to say it can please the senses, touch the heart, and elevate the soul, but can never arouse the imagination or suggest an idea to the mind.

There is an argument in the minds of many, and one which it is quite difficult to answer—that such works in any branch of art are worthiest, indeed that such alone are perfect as appeal simultaneously to man's entire complex nature, which quicken harmoniously all his diverse faculties; that is, which at once gratify the senses, stir the emotions, arouse the intellect, excite the imagination, and inspire the soul; which strike the full chord of humanity, if we may so express it, rather than draw vibrations from a single string. The true wisdom for the musician is to ignore neither the potency of single note melodies nor the infinite diversity of chord effects, but to possess facile and masterly command of both.   Edw. Baxter Perry.

57. Feb. 26th.

Music gives birth to aspiration. It makes a true man truer; it makes a bad man better. UPTON.

58.
Many-sided Music. Feb. 27th.

It is impossible to love in equal degree all forms of music, yet it is necessary to know many. One may have a special relish for Chopin, but he will not comprehend that lurid and wavering genius without also knowing works which differ widely from Chopin, such as those of Mendelssohn and Beethoven. One may delight in the animated rhythms and clear but abstruse harmonizations of Bach, yet he would be, of a truth, a dry musician if he found not pleasure in the rich, sensuous effects of Schumann, in the dazzling technique of Liszt, in the dreamy melancholy of Schubert, in the heroic and pathetic grandeurs of Beethoven, in the captivating tunefulness of Mozart. J. S. VAN CLEVE.

59. Feb. 28th.

Music revives the recollections it would appease.
MME. DE STAËL.

60.
Art for the Poor. Feb. 29th.

I believe that art is not a luxury for the rich, but a necessity for the poor. I believe that it is necessary to stimulate the mind engrossed with the sordid care of eking out a material existence. The spirit gladly follows the flight of the imagination, for thus and thus only can it leave behind its troubles and cares. I believe that, of all the arts, music is the best language in which to express an ideal. I believe that music is the natural language in which a people expresses its ideals, its emotions, its character. The folk-songs of the various races of Europe prove this. I believe that this language should be taught to all, in order that all may be able to express their true feelings. Words may lie—music cannot. I believe that all people can learn to sing. FRANK DAMROSCH.

61.
March 1st. **Incentive to Piety.**

Music, the daughter rather than the imitator of Nature, impelling us to pious thought by its solemn, mysterious accents, appeals directly to our feelings, and is mistress of our deepest emotions. WEBER.

March 2d. ### 62.

Music is the first, the simplest, the most effective of all instruments of moral instruction. RUSKIN.

63.
March 3d. **Music as Pleasure.**

No one, unless he is very one-sided, will deny that one of the missions of music is to furnish simple pleasure, or enjoyment that requires no particular thought. It is no slight mission to supply a relaxation to tired minds, nerves, and muscles—a relaxation that is in itself perfectly harmless, no matter in what quantity it be taken. "Music is the only sensual pleasure without vice." This being true, and I think no one will question it, we may say that did music have no higher mission than simply to divert and to rest tired humanity, or to occupy in a harmless way those who might otherwise be engaged in that which is not harmless, mankind should rise up and call it blessed.

W. F. GATES.

64.
No Dearth of Literature. March 4th.

The abundance of musical literature is the delight of its ripened scholars, the despair of the half ripe, and the dazzlement of the eager beginner. One begins by resolving to know everything, soon he despairs of knowing anything, at last he is glad to know something.

J. S. VAN CLEVE.

65.
Intellect Plus Emotion. March 5th.

Music is, in its nature, that one of the fine arts which has for its material musical tones. It affords us enjoyment on its lowest plane through the discrimination of refined from coarse tones and by combinations and contrasts of different qualities of tone. The pleasure thus derived is refined, but it is sensuous merely. Music adds to this very high intellectual enjoyment. In its more elaborate forms, such as the fugue, the sonata, the symphony, the music-drama, it taxes the intellectual resources of both composer and student in equal degree with the greatest intellectual productions of the human mind in other fields of activity. It thus adds intellectual to sensuous enjoyment, and so ranks high in the scale of mental activities.

But its primary and ultimate function is to express, convey, and excite feeling. To this the sensuous and intellectual elements are subordinate. The imagination reaches its highest flights and performs its most legitimate function when it deals with its musical materials in their relation to emotion.

JOHN C. FILLMORE.

66.

March 6th.   **Supernal Beauty.**

It is in music, perhaps, that the soul most nearly attains the great end for which, when inspired by the poetic sentiment, it struggles—the creation of supernal beauty. It *may* be, indeed, that here this sublime end is now and then attained *in fact*. We are often made to feel, with a shivering delight, that from an earthly harp are stricken notes which *cannot* have been unfamiliar to the angels.   EDGAR ALLEN POE.

67.

March 7th.   **The All-sufficiency of Music.**

I think sometimes could I only have music on my own terms, could I live in a great city, and know where I could go whenever I wished the ablution and inundation of musical waves, that were a bath and a medicine.   EMERSON.

March 8th.   68.

My language is understood all over the world.

HAYDN.

March 9th.   69.

Music commonly goes hand in hand with kindness.

HENRY T. FINCK.

70.

March 10th.   **Sweet Pleasure.**

I need not tell you that music bears upon its wings some of the sweetest and purest pleasures of the passing hour, whether it gushes forth from the human lips or from the breath of old Æolus upon his throne. Music elevates and quickens our perceptions; it softens and subdues the rebellious dispositions; it refines and soothes the wayward and turbulent passions; it nerves the heart to deeds of valor and heroism; it gives joy and consolation in the hour of affliction, and carries the soul captive across the rough and stormy sea of life, and pierces beyond the vale of time to welcome, with angelic voice, the wandering spirit to its final end.

Unlike most branches of education it becomes useful immediately, for it cultivates the mind, body, and soul, and in the whole curriculum of school studies there is not one which can do more; for, when studied rightly, it becomes a means of mental discipline, over which mathematics, with all its boasted glory, can claim no superiority. A singer will at once acknowledge that no problem in arithmetic calls for a keener appreciation of the faculties than does singing or playing at sight a difficult piece of music. AUGUST DOERNER.

71.
To Every Mood. March 11th.

Music, like other arts, appeals primarily to the emotional side of our nature; responds to our every mood, grieving with our sorrow, rejoicing at our joy, lending her aid to interpret thoughts and feelings that would otherwise lack expression. Many, indeed, to whom Music is known only under this aspect, fail altogether to realize that in order to appreciate all her charms fully, she must be looked at from other points of view. RIDLEY PRENTICE.

72.
March 12th. **Beyond.**

It will be in and through music that human thought will be carried beyond the point it has hitherto reached.

SHORTHOUSE.

73.
March 13th. **The Highest Reason for Musical Study.**

Though a man's life may not be prolonged, it may be widened and deepened by what he puts into it; and any possibility of bringing people into touch with those highest moments in art in which great ideals were realized, in music in which noble aspirations and noble sentiments were embodied, is a chance of enriching human experience in the noblest manner, and the humanizing influences which democracy may hereafter have at its disposal may thereby be infinitely enlarged.

C. H. H. PARRY.

74.
March 14th. **Music in the Air.**

Music was, from the beginning of the world, given by God to all and every creature, and created with all from the beginning, for there is nothing in the world which doth not give from itself a sound. Yea, even the air which is in itself invisible and incomprehensible, in which there seemeth to be the least music, that is the least beautiful sound, and which appeareth quite mute and silent, if it be moved and driven through anything, it giveth its own music, its own sound; and that which was before mute, now beginneth to have a voice, and to become music, that it may be heard and comprehended, although it was not heard and comprehended before, and through it doth the spirit reveal great and marvellous secrets, whereof I will not speak at this present. MARTIN LUTHER.

75.

Three Elements. March 15th.

Three elements may be distinguished in music—the emotional, the imaginative, and the fanciful.

The first is pre-eminently human, expressive of our relations to God and men; the second is descriptive, yet not of things—*i. e.*, objects of nature and art—but of the impression we receive from them; the last of the three is best characterized by the definition which Leigh Hunt gives of fancy: it is " the younger sister of imagination, without the other's weight of thought and feeling." FRIEDRICH NIECKS.

76. March 16th

Singing is all we know they do above. WALLER.

77.

Extension of Musical Knowledge. March 17th.

It is a pleasure to observe what an increasing amount of attention periodical literature is giving to music. The popular and standard magazines are competing with one another in their articles about our art. The daily and weekly papers are giving more and more space to musical affairs, and even some college professors brag about not " knowing one tune from another " less than formerly. Business men now have to acknowledge that musicians are proving themselves to be sufficiently business-like in their affairs to keep even with the world, and at least tolerate the musician where but a few years ago they openly showed contempt. Some of the theological seminaries now have vocal music taught to the students who are preparing to "regulate" the music of our churches. But why so many ministers should know theology and not music, and still think themselves fitted for their profession is past finding out. School trustees are seeing the value of vocal music as a study for the preparation of boys and girls for the duties of useful and happy citizenship. In some communities it has even come to pass that a musician who behaves himself as well as other men is considered a "fellow-citizen." ANON.

78.

March 18th.   **Beauty.**

The highest value of music lies in the fact that it embodies in forms which powerfully appeal to us those great principles of order, harmony, proportion, variety in unity—in a word, beauty. The kind of study which is of the most service to us is that which enables us to perceive and absorb these principles. Plato says that "he who has music in his soul will be most in love with the loveliest." This is the secret of the highest culture. Devotion to what is beautiful— that is, to what is truly beautiful, not merely pretty— is in every way ennobling. Love and admiration worthily bestowed are the means of growth to the soul.

The great thing, then, is to get music into the soul. How is this to be done? Surely not by pursuing it as an accomplishment or a means of amusement. Music must be studied as a literature. We must make ourselves acquainted with the thoughts of the great composers, and fill our minds with the images of beauty which they have created. This should be the aim of every teacher and pupil. We should cultivate a wise discrimination between what is great and excellent and what is trivial. The great music of the world is alone worthy of prolonged study. Trifles have their place in life, but we give them much attention at our peril.

BERTRAM C. HENRY.

79.
Room for Improvement.   March 19th.

It is an instinct of childhood and of happiness to express itself in music; so the laborer whistles the questionable street-song, the child lisps her kindergarten songs, while the sister sings the music she is taught in the higher school grades. The point is, are these school-songs in general of a nature high enough above the common street-songs to warrant a hope for the sufficient advance of musical culture through this, its most powerful agent?

ANON.

80.
A Glorious Gift.   March 20th.

Music is a beautiful and glorious gift of God; the reflection of the heavenly harmonies in which His angels and all the celestial host ever praise and glorify their Creator, singing in sweet strains: "Holy, holy, holy, Lord God of Sabaoth!"

MICHAEL PRAETORIUS.

81.
Cheerfulness.   March 21st.

Song brings of itself a cheerfulness that wakes the heart to joy.

EURIPIDES.

82.
March 22d.   Music Suggestive.

Musical literature covers a field of genius, intelligence, and emotion. Hardly a thought which the mind of man has conceived but has been focused and set to music. Music suggests everything. It is where thought takes a leap beyond the humanly definite scope of ideas that the language of music is needed to express it. Music suggests all that is subtle and divine to the imagination, and even when it appeals most vividly one knows that a thousand minds interpret it differently. Think, then, what a kingdom of riches lies within the musician's grasp. And the keynote to this kingdom is a perfect technic. "Music is well said to be like the speech of angels." "God is its author. He laid the keystone of all harmonies. He planned all perfect combinations, and He made us so that we could hear and understand."   Mrs. Sherwood.

83.
March 23d.   Song Universal.

In society, where education requires a submission to rule, singing belongs to the domain of art; but in a primitive state, all nations have their songs. Musical rhythm drives away weariness, lessens fatigue, detaches the mind from the painful realities of life, and braces up the courage to meet danger. Soldiers march to their war-songs; the laborer rests, listening to a joyous carol; in the solitary chamber the needle-woman accompanies her work with some love-ditty; and in divine worship the heart is raised above earthly things by the solemn chant.   Anon.

84.
Perfection. March 24th.

Music is the wondrous perfection, the highest height of that expression, a reach so far above the daily level that only by transcending earthly capacity could we interpret its burden. — CHAS. G. WHITING.

85.
A Soul Gymnastic. March 25th.

As gymnastic exercise is necessary to keep the body healthy, musical exercise is necessary to keep the soul healthy; and the proper nourishment of the intellect and passions can no more take place without music than the proper functions of the stomach and blood can go on without exercise. — RUSKIN.

86.
Music Moves the Heart. March 26th.

Music has been called the speech of angels, and it is a beautiful fancy which ascribes to these pure beings such a method of communication. But let us be thankful that music is not monopolized by the angels; mortals may share in its delights; mortals also may speak its language.

There is a certain peculiarity of the language of music which distinguishes it from all the other languages of man. They appeal to the intellect of man; if they reach and move his heart it is through the intellect. It is only through the mind that words affect the heart. Music, however, appeals immediately to our emotions. It stirs up within us feelings that words could not awaken; it rouses us to action by its own immediate power.

Take a little ballad, telling the story of some life—a gem in its way—expressed as beautifully as words can express anything, and let it be read in any circle; and though the beauty of the verse may touch some hearts, the effect will not be very noticeable. But set the same ballad to a plaintive air, and let some sweet voice sing it, and you shall see tears starting into the eyes of half the company. It was the music that went to the heart and carried with it some pulses of the pathos with which the poetry was surcharged.

WASHINGTON GLADDEN, D.D.

87.

March 27th. **As an Educator.**

Music is one of the greatest educators in the world; and the study of it in its highest departments, such as composition, harmony, and counterpoint, develops the mind as much as the study of mathematics or the languages. It teaches us love, kindness, charity, perseverance, patience, diligence, promptness, and punctuality.

ANON.

88.

March 28th. **A Strange Bird.**

Music is a thing of the soul; a rose-lipped shell that murmurs of the eternal sea; a strange bird singing the songs of another shore.

J. G. HOLLAND.

89.

March 29th. **Music and Love.**

What love is to man, music is to the arts and to mankind. Music is love itself—it is the purest, most ethereal language of passion, showing in a thousand ways all possible changes of color and feeling; and though only true in a single instance, it can yet be understood by thousands of men—who all feel differently.

C. M. VON WEBER.

90. March 30th.

The love of music seems to exist for its own sake.

HERBERT SPENCER.

91.
Music a Necessity of Nature. March 31st.

Darwin says: "Neither the enjoyment nor the capacity of producing musical notes are faculties of the least direct use to man in reference to his ordinary habits of life." Physiologically he may be correct, but as soon as mere rudimentary actions are left, and existence becomes life, his statement is completely false. Indeed, music is, as this philosopher elsewhere says, bound up in daily life, and a necessity of existence. Of its usefulness in daily life there can be no question. What would religious services be without organs and singing? What would armies be without bands? If music were a luxury, would people spend so much time and money on it? It is not to obtain mere ear-enjoyment; it is because it is a *necessity* to satisfy certain requirements of the mind. It enters into the chemistry of the mind as salt does into the chemistry of the body. Here and there you will meet with a person who says, "I never eat salt—I do not require it." Well, you are sorry for him. There is evidently something wrong in his physical constitution. So when anyone assumes a tone of lofty superiority, and boasts that he knows nothing about music, and pretends not to be able to distinguish one tune from another, you may either accept his statement with some reserve, or conclude that there is something wrong in his physical or mental faculties, and recommend an aurist.

ARTHUR SULLIVAN.

92.

April 1st.　　　**In Mysterious Tones.**

Music remains the universal language of nature; it speaks to us in wonderful and mysterious tones; in vain do we try to retain its effect by signs—for any artificial connecting of the hieroglyphs results, after all, in *indicating* the idea of that which we have heard.

HOFFMANN.

93.

April 2d.　　　**Permanency of the Best.**

The best music, like the best painting, is entirely popular; it at once commends itself to everyone, and does so through all ages. The worst music, like the worst painting, commends itself at first, in like manner, to ninety-nine people out of a hundred, but after doing them its appointed quantity of mischief, it is forgotten, and new modes of mischief composed.　　RUSKIN.

94.

April 3d.　　　**A Product of the Imagination.**

Music first comes into being as an idea in the mind of the composer; it is the product of his imagination. And the real composition is what the composer hears in imagination. All attempt at performance are efforts to represent this idea in actual sound, and are necessarily only approximations. In order for the listener to hear the real composition, the sounds heard with the outward ear must stimulate his imagination to activity similar to that which originally went on in the composer's mind. Then those deeper powers of the soul, over which we have no direct control, will be aroused to sympathetic activity, and the full significance of the composition, both intellectual and emotional, will be comprehended. BERTRAM C. HENRY.

95.
A Rule of Life. April 4th.

Music is such a perfect expression of human emotion that we can almost deduce from it a moral science—a rule of life. Every thought which arises out of any cause is expressed in music, because music is innate and spontaneous. Thus the musical composer is truer and less disguised than he who expresses his thoughts in words. If there are imperfections in his nature, he does not seek, like the mental philosopher, to omit or conceal them; he leaves them, with his virtues, as a part of himself; and since no man is free from fault, we find more real life and congeniality in music and are more inclined, under its influences, to acknowledge our vices or failings. GOODRICH.

96.
Pleasure in Art. April 5th.

It is only when our feelings, our mind, and our taste derive full satisfaction from music that our pleasure in art really begins. Those who delight in the mere concord of sounds are incapable of deeper appreciation.
F. HILLER.

97.

April 6th.   **Our Reasons for Singing.**

After you have learned to reason, young people, of course you will be very grave, if not dull, you think. By no means anything of the kind. After learning to reason, you will learn to sing, for you will want to. There is so much reason for singing in the sweet world, when one thinks rightly of it; none for grumbling, provided always you have entered in at the strait gate. You will sing all along the road then, in a little while, in a manner pleasant for other people to hear.

RUSKIN.

April 7th.   98.

While the painter or sculptor must borrow the raiment for his idea from the human form or landscape, the musician is alone with his imagination.

HUEFFER.

99.

April 8th.   **Subtle Music.**

It is a strange thing, the subtle form and conditions of music. When the composer has conceived it in his mind, it is not there; when he has committed it to paper, it is not there; when he has called together his orchestra and choristers from the north and south, it is there, but it is gone again when they disappear. It has always, as it were, put on immortality afresh. It is forever being born anew—born, indeed, to die and leave dead notes and dumb instruments behind.

LADY EASTLAKE.

100.   April 9th.

Music is a higher manifestation than all wisdom and philosophy.   BEETHOVEN.

101.

Antiquity of Music.   April 10th.

Music is as old as the world itself. In some form or other it has always existed. Ere man learned to give vent to his emotions in tuneful voice, Nature, animate and inaminate, under the hand of the Great Master, sang his praises. Of this we learn in the sacred writings; while all about us are the songs of birds, the musical sighing of the winds, the fall of waters, and the many forms of the music of Nature, we have palpable evidence of its present existence, and assurances of its remote antiquity. It would seem that not long after "God breathed into the nostrils of man the breath of life and he became a living soul," he learned to express the joys and yearnings of his soul in song first, then with some sort of musical instrument. And to man it was given, commencing with the early ages, to develop the simple ejaculations or melodies of a praise-giving soul into a beautiful, a noble art, replete at times with harmonic intricacies, and again with melodies, grand in their very simplicity; into a beneficent science, divine from its inception, which has ever had as votaries many of earth's greatest minds, and has become a fountain of delight to all mankind.

                                               TROTTER.

102.

For Love, Not Command.   April 11th.

People send me poems to set to music. This seems to me like sending one a girl to fall in love with. One happens to read a poem, it touches one, and then one sets it to music. One happens to see a girl, she pleases one, and one falls in love with her. But both spontaneously, not by command. RUBINSTEIN.

103.
April 12th. **To Soothe and Soften.**

Oh, surely melody from Heaven was sent to cheer the soul when tired with human strife, to soothe the wayward heart by sorrow rent, and soften down the rugged road of life! KIRKE WHITE.

104.
April 13th. **Cultivated Enjoyment.**

I am convinced that many who think they have no taste for music would learn to appreciate it and partake of its blessings, if they often listened to good instrumental music with earnestness and attention.
FERDINAND HILLER.

105.
April 14th. **Music Cultivates Our Better Natures.**

How little there is of tenderness, of fervor, of enthusiasm, of sympathy, in the average middle-aged American in these latter days of the nineteenth century, and yet how wholly we ignore this lack in our lives and in our systems of education! Music is the only study followed by us which arouses and intensifies the emotions, and so gives us development in this direction. Whatever may have been claimed as to the variety of mental and moral types among the great musicians, this may indisputably be said, that there never was a callous or barren emotional nature among them all.

Singular, but true, it is, that while music appeals to the better class of feelings as does nothing else, it has little or no power to arouse the uglier emotions. Tears have been started, hearts softened, sorrows soothed, patriotism kindled, tenderness aroused, courage steeled, religion deepened, aspiration awakened by music often; but there never was and never can be written a strain of music which would excite the passions of greed, avarice, gluttony, anger, or envy in the listener.

EDW. BAXTER PERRY.

106.
In the Heart of Man. April 15th.

What a marvellous thing is music! How little are we able to fathom its deep mysteries! And yet does it not live in the very heart of man? does it not so imbue him with its grace and beauty that his mind is wholly engrossed by it; that another and purer life seems to raise him above the shadows and miseries here on earth? HOFFMANN.

107.
The Divine Organist. April 16th.

Many mighty harmonies have been discoursed by instruments that had been dumb or discordant but that God knew their stops. RUSKIN.

108.
Realism. April 17th.

Absolute music is confessedly the highest form of that art; yet there is hardly a composer who has not given moments of extraneous interest to even his most serious works, some literary quality of motive, or some picturesque effect of incident. In the popular hearing, such things heighten the pleasure of the music in the same way that situation strengthens drama, plot intensifies the interest of fiction, and episode enhances the enjoyment of a picture. ANON.

April 18th. 109.

Music is to the mind as is air to the body.
PLATO.

110.

April 19th. **Intellect Subordinate to Emotion.**

The highest art is the art that touches the soul most deeply; the art that is most intense in healthful spiritual power; the art of Beethoven; the art of the Sonata Appassionata. Therefore, if it is the purpose of music to touch the emotional nature, you miss the meaning entirely if you content yourself with the merely interesting variety of the tones produced. One may listen to musical sounds as he gazes at an intricate piece of machinery. His intellect is excited to a certain extent by the complex character of the piece. But intellectual delight in music is a very small part of the joy that the true listener should derive. In music the intellectual is made subordinate to the emotional. Music never was intended as a language of the intellect. If its intellectual character were its highest quality, then music would take a low rank when compared with many other studies. But music is the supreme language of the higher sensibilities, unequalled in all the realm of emotional speech. Herbert Spencer says that, considered as the language of emotion, "Music is only second in importance to the languages of the intellect—perhaps not second."

Purely intellectual compositions, however interesting they may be, are not, properly, music. If Bach was, as some imagine him to be, a purely intellectual writer, he could not properly be called a musician. But Bach is full of deep emotional meaning, and the successful student must find it and feel its thrill.

E. E. AYRES.

111.
Songless Women. April 20th.

A woman who cannot sing is a flower without perfume. There may come a time when a weary little head lies on its mother's bosom; little eyelids are drooping, twilight is drawing about her—too early for a lamp, too early for any but little folks to sleep; then it is that all the accomplishments of her girlhood are as nothing compared with one simple song that lulls a tired baby to sleep.

M. B. ANDERSON.

112.
These Not from Music. April 21st.

I would appeal to any man, whether ever he found himself urged to acts of selfishness, cruelty, treachery, revenge, or malevolence, by the power of musical sounds; or if he ever found jealousy, suspicion, or ingratitude engendered in his breast, either from harmony or discord?

CHARLES AVISON.

113. April 22d.

Music produces like effects on the mind as good medicine on the body.

MIRANDOLA.

114.
April 23d.   **Joy, not Sadness.**

Music is a spirit. I have seen a mother at her work and a farm-boy at his task, and as I heard them humming snatches of song, I have said music lightens labor. I have heard that martial music urges the soldier to battle, and I have affirmed that music inspires patriotism. I have heard that beasts have been charmed by its delicious sounds, and I have reasoned that music quells passion. It does more; it suggests ideas; it quickens the imagination; it dispels sadness; it adds to joy. Music is the only perfect language of all the higher emotions.   J. G. ABBOTT.

115.
April 24th.   **Superior Emotional Endowment.**

The love of music, whether one ever studies it or not, is always an inevitable sign of superior emotional endowment, and listening to music with real appreciation arouses, exercises, and so develops the emotional nature in its finest and highest phases. As we listen, with swelling hearts but tranquil souls, we feel ourselves lifted, warmed, refreshed, and are conscious that the spirit within us quickens the insensate clod which confines it.   EDW. BAXTER PERRY.

April 25th.   116.

Singing is one preparation for heaven.   BEVAN.

117.
April 26th.   **Music as Mediator.**

Music is the mediator between the spiritual and sensual life; although the spirit be not master of that which it creates through music, yet it is blessed in this recreation, which, like every creation of art, is mightier than the artist. BEETHOVEN.

118. April 27th.

Music is almost all we have of heaven on earth.
BEETHOVEN.
ADDISON.

119.

Music is Revealed Beauty. April 28th.

Every true work of art is a revelation of beauty, a message which was transmitted through the mind of the artist, but did not in strictness originate there, the expression of a vision of something beyond the limits of ordinary human life. Music is in no wise behind her sister arts in this respect. Think for a moment what are the elements of music—rhythm, harmony, and melody. The first of these is a universal law of motion; it symbolizes symmetry, proportion, that living balance of forces which makes varied, yet consistent, activity possible. Again, what ideas does harmony suggest: the existence of many in one, the relation of parts to the whole, the principle which governs the constitution of every organism—man, the State, the solar system, the universe. And melody brings in addition a charm which melts the heart, calling forth its deepest admiration, its truest love. All this may be discerned in music. In this art the discoveries of science, the divinations of philosophy, the moral aspirations of religion, all find a parallel, not as abstractions, but as glowing concrete realities, which "find their way into the secret places of the soul," arousing its fullest activity, and making themselves part of the very nature of the sincere lover of music.

BERTRAM C. HENRY.

120.

April 29th.   **Vitality Through Music.**

Music is not an alcohol to intoxicate the musician, an anodyne to bring mere momentary forgetfulness of the day's cares and troubles, nor a sense-killing potion to waft him lazily into luxurious hasheesh-dreams of a Mahomet's Paradise; it brings with it the wholesome oxygen necessary to his complete vitality. So soon as he is in the presence of a mighty composition, he plunges *into* the music, heart and soul, and his whole being is aroused to vigorous action.

W. F. APTHORP.

April 30th.   121.

It is music's lofty mission to shed light on the depths of the human heart.   SCHUMANN.

122.

May 1st.   **Great Art from Great Nations.**

The Greeks knew the value of music as a social agent, for Plutarch tells us the sweet singer Therpander was sent to the Island of Lesbos to calm by his voice a tumultuous uprising. Cicero and Napoleon agree that music can change the feelings and conditions of a state, and that legislators should give it, of all arts, the greatest encouragement.

Great art always comes with broad national feelings, as in the ages of Pericles, Augustus, and Elizabeth. There is a pertinent coincidence in the fact that Germany is at once the most musical nation and the one possessing the highest social efficiency.   WM. BENBOW.

123.   May 2d.

Music would not need to exist if one could represent by speech or by painting what it expresses.

F. Hiller.

124.

Music is Real.   May 3d.

Music is not an accident; it is not the result of an abnormal or unnatural emotional state. It is an organic growth like the flowers or the trees. A musical idea is a real idea; not, as many people suppose, an evanescent or even accidental combination of sounds of different pitch and quality; and the fact that it sounds through time, instead of existing in space as do the painters' or architects' or sculptors' ideas, does not make it any the less tangible or any the less permanent.

The musical idea is a fact, and its function, like any other artistic or poetic idea, is the expression of truth and beauty. And just in proportion as it does express the beautiful and the true does it have life, health, and longevity.   George W. Chadwick.

125.

Intellect vs. Emotional Music.   May 4th.

Music changes from age to age, and in these very changes lies its strength, for it changes only as our conditions of mind and life change, but this fact remains forever immutable. Music that is wholly emotional is unhealthy and morbid; music that is entirely intellectual is dull; and the only music that stands the test of the ages is that in which the intellectual and the emotional are held in just equipoise. And Bach, Mozart, Beethoven, and Wagner all have recognized this unwritten law of our art, and have acted upon it.

Louis C. Elson.

126.

May 5th. Its Elevating Power.

Music, properly understood, may become a potent force for good, because it furnishes the only medium of expression in which may successfully be embodied those transitory, exalted, supersensuous moods and feelings which come to us all rarely, in our best moments, and are more frequent and familiar to the really artistic temperament, but which even the language of the poets confessedly fails to express. The best music deals most exclusively with these intangible phases of experience, and constant familiarity with so pure and lofty a form of expression, and with the softening, elevating, ennobling moods and sentiments which are its proper subject-matter, must tend to lift and refine, as well as to broaden and deepen the heart and life of the student. A man is not only known, he is in a large measure formed, by the company he keeps, and daily companionship with genius in its highest moments, as embodied in these art works, cannot fail to have its effect.

Edw. Baxter Perry.

127.

May 6th. As No Other Can Do.

Music inspires, enrages, elevates, saddens, cheers, and soothes the soul as no other one of the arts can do.

George P. Upton.

128.
Both Specialize and Generalize. May 7th.

Goethe said, "A man acquires a new soul with each new language that he learns." He also said, "A man is better for every good song that he hears," and Goethe was the originator of a pretty bit of catachresis used by George Sand, and often quoted since, to the effect that "architecture is frozen music." It is so obvious as to scarcely need statement, much less elaborate proof, that music is something more than mechanism, and that he who would sound its depths must have a fathoming line of prolonged collateral study, and must attach to this line a plummet-ball of intellect somewhat weightier than a feather. Those who have sharp-cut and compact diamonds of antithetic aphorism may consider the following: "An educated man should know everything of something, and something of everything." The musician, like any other intellectual worker in literature, science, art, should specialize and generalize both with judgment. Let him not only adopt one particular instrument, but let him work in the literature of that instrument some definite and peculiar vein, the one most cognate to his special gifts; but let him enrich his mind the while with suggestions of the widest intellectual amplitude. The star that shimmers in a dewdrop is inconceivably remote. J. S. VAN CLEVE.

129.
The Influence of Music. May 8th.

It is the problem of the arts to represent life. Every painting, every piece of statuary, every poem, every representation on the stage gives us a piece of life, a representation of ourselves and our passions. Music does the same, only to a much higher degree. But, says Schopenhauer, while the other arts give us a picture, a mere representation of life, music gives us life *itself*; that is, music speaks so true, in such powerful terms, it pictures our feelings so correctly, that the heart yields irresistibly to it, and that it affects us much more powerfully than other arts. But while the arts give us a picture or a representation of life, while music speaks the truest language of life, it leaves the interpretation of this language to ourselves.

KARL MERZ.

130.
May 9th.   **A Reliable Guide.**

Music is a great, and in many respects a reliable guide in the study of human progress and development.

FREDERIC L. RITTER.

May 10th.   131.

Music washes away from the soul the dust of every-day life. AUERBACH.

132.
May 11th.   **A Mental Stimulus.**

Beyond necessitating much mental activity in its acquirement and production, music is, in its turn, a stimulant to mental activity. Not only does the fire of old thought burn brightly, but new thought bursts into active flame, though before it had lingered dormant like the flickering blue light that hovers o'er the slowly-burning coals.

As we voice our emotions in music, they vivify into

definite being thoughts that had been lingering on the threshold of consciousness, and which needed but the spark of related emotion to awaken them into life. And it is with emotion as with thought: One emotion induces another, and each is the germ of thought concepts, actions, and deeds which may culminate in results beyond calculation. W. F. GATES.

133.
Begin in Childhood. May 12th.

The study of music, rightly pursued, benefits the student both morally and intellectually in a high degree. It is consequently worthy of all the furtherance which home influence can give it. Moreover, there are things of the greatest importance which can be learned easily at the time when the child is most dependent upon immediate family surroundings, but with greater difficulty and expense at the age when the pupil usually comes to the teacher. Many a man vainly wishes he were able to comprehend and enjoy music who might easily have gained the power had he been subjected to the right influence in childhood.

BERTRAM C. HENRY.

134.
Ignorance Should Humiliate. May 13th.

It ought to be expected of educated men that they will be as humiliated to have to acknowledge ignorance of Beethoven and Schumann and their works, as of Shakespeare and Shelley and theirs.

H. E. KREHBIEL.

135.

May 14th.   **Emotional Discipline.**

The habitual exercise and discipline of the emotions, as, for example, in music or acting, is not the ruin of, but the very condition of moral health.

H. R. HAWEIS.

136.

May 15th.   **The Most Effectual Art.**

Music has been a sort of religion to me all my life; and if ever in my closing days I can be proud of anything, it will be that I have during my long life always endeavored to serve the cause of music, and to serve it well. Music has influences beyond those of any other art. I do not think that by the sight of an admirable picture, or an admirable piece of statuary, crowds of people will ever be so moved as by the strains of music. It has a great softening influence upon the large mass of the people.   SIR CHARLES HALLE.

137.

May 16th.   **Not Very Dangerous to Morals.**

Music is the only sensual qualification which mankind may indulge in to excess without injury to their moral or religious feelings.   ADDISON.

138.

May 17th.   **The Nature of Music.**

Music may be defined as the art of producing emotions by combinations of sound. It is not on the human species alone that the power of this art is felt. The greater part of organized beings are more or less under its influence. The sense of hearing, on which it acts immediately, seems to be its only agent; its power is most developed on the nervous system, and hence the variety of its effects. It is not the ear alone which is affected by music. If music unites certain qualities, it produces emotion, in an indeterminate manner, indeed, but more powerfully than painting, sculpture, or any other art. FRANCIS J. FETIS.

139.
Music Develops Character. May 18th.

Here is where the great use of music comes in. It develops character, it adds to life. Knowing how it acts, one can see to it that it acts only upon right affections, impulses, emotions. Remember, it does not give; it develops. It will work upon just those passions and emotions presented to it, and no others. It is needless, then, to say further what should be done to get the best results. ANON.

140. May 19th.

Music is a universal language, frequently mispronounced and broken up into rude dialects. ANON.

141.
Exceeded Only by Metaphysics. May 20th.

Music should be made an elective, a fit substitute for any other study. There are college professors who claim that music is an easy study, and not an equivalent of others found in the curriculum. Let me invite you to try this study, take up music as an art and as a science, and in a year's time you will acknowledge that there is not a branch now taught in a university, metaphysics excepted, that presents more peculiar difficulties, that needs longer time for complete mastery, than the subjects of harmony, counterpoint, and musical composition. KARL MERZ.

May 21st. 142.

The life that is in tune with the melodies of heaven cannot fail of being happy. J. H. SHORTHOUSE.

143.

May 22d. **The Arts Compared.**

"Music is an elegant art, and a fine amusement, but, as an occupation it hath little dignity, having for its object mere entertainment and pleasure." So wrote the venerable Dr. Handel, father of the composer, two centuries ago, and this feeling against music as a profession has been held by many, even to the present time, and musicians have to contend against it everywhere. That this is an erroneous view to take of an art requiring such an expenditure of time, money, and strength by those who are its representatives, will become more and more apparent as its beauties are better appreciated by the public generally. Music has the power to develop as much poetry and delicacy of feeling as painting, sculpture, or the other fine arts, and, when its tones are combined by the master-hand of genius, to create as great monuments of skill as those produced by a Raphael, a Phidias, or a Shakespeare.

What is there in painting greater than Mozart's Requiem, Haydn's Creation, or Glück's operas?

What is there in sculpture grander than Bach's Passion Music, or Handel's Messiah?

What is there in architecture that surpasses Beethoven's Nine Symphonies?

What is there in literature to equal Wagner's sublime music-dramas? L. R. CHURCH.

144. May 23d.

Music once admitted to the soul becomes a sort of spirit, and never dies; it wanders perturbedly through the halls and galleries of the memory, and is often heard again, distinct and living as when it first displaced the wavelets of the air. BULWER-LYTTON.

145.
Music a Healer. May 24th.

Music will some day become a powerful and acknowledged therapeutic. . . . There are moods of exhausted feeling in which certain kinds of music would act like poison. There are other kinds of music which soothe and—if I may use the word—lubricate the worn ways of the nervous centres. You will ask, what music is good for that? We reply, judgment and common-sense, and, above all, sympathy, affectional and musical sympathy, will partly be your guide: but experience must decide. H. R. HAWEIS.

146.
Not to be Defined. May 25th.

To define the precise functions of music, and fix its place in a scheme of fine arts, has proved one of the most intricate problems in that intricate science, æsthetics. JAMES LULLY.

147.

May 26th.   A Serious Matter.

Music for me, you must know, is a very solemn matter; so solemn that I do not feel myself justified in trying to adapt it to any subject that does not touch me, heart and soul.   MENDELSSOHN.

148.

May 27th.   Music the Nurse of the Soul.

I would fain know what music is. I seek it as a man seeks eternal wisdom. Yesterday evening I walked, late in the moonlight, in the beautiful avenue of lime-trees on the bank of the Rhine; and I heard a tapping noise and soft singing. At the door of a cottage, under the blooming lime-tree, sat a mother and her twin babies; the one lay at her breast, the other in a cradle, which she rocked with her foot, keeping time to her singing. In the very germ, then, when the first trace of life begins to stir, music is the nurse of the soul; it murmurs in the ear and the child sleeps; the tones are the companions of his dreams; they are the world in which he lives. He has nothing; the babe although cradled in his mother's arms is alone in the spirit: but tones find entrance into the half-conscious soul, and nourish it as the earth nourishes the life of plants.   BERTINI.

149.

May 28th.   From the Cradle to the Grave.

Life is one great symphony. From the cradle to the grave one finds in music an expression of his highest, richest, divinest life. Music lulls the infant to peaceful slumbers; by its aid the lover wooes and wins the maiden of his choice. Music heightens the joy of the wedding; stimulates the flagging footsteps of the soldier in the weary march; is the expression of joy and thankfulness for the harvest season; aids by its voice the merrymaking after toil; glides with healing sympathy into the funeral rites; and in death, had we but ears to hear, the music from the other world might roll in upon us and resolve in heavenly harmonies all discords of earth's jangling life. LYMAN ABBOTT.

150.
Virtue in Music. May 29th.

There is no doubt that the seed of many virtues is in such hearts as are devoted to music; those who are not touched by music I hold to be like stocks and stones. LUTHER.

151.
Music Criticism. May 30th.

How seldom do we meet with a proper amount of sympathy and knowledge, honesty and courage, in a critic—four qualities which he ought to possess. It is therefore very sad for the realm of music that criticism, in so many respects so useful, should often be the occupation of heads by no means gifted with these qualities. BACH.

152.
Music and Love. May 31st.

If our noble art of music does not cease to elevate and delight us despite all its abuses, it is only a proof of its great and eternal glory—it is just so with love.

HILLER.

153.

June 1st.   **It Refines and Soothes.**

I need not tell you that music bears upon its wings some of the sweetest and purest pleasures of the passing hour, whether it gushes forth from the human lips or from the breath of old Æolus upon his throne. Music elevates and quickens our perceptions; it softens and subdues the rebellious disposition; it refines and soothes the wayward and turbulent passions; it nerves the heart to deeds of valor and heroism; it gives joy and consolation in the hour of affliction, and carries the soul captive across the rough and stormy sea of life, and stands beyond the vale of time to welcome with angelic voice, the wandering spirit to its final home.

Dr. John Hall.

154.

June 2d.   **A Voice from the Eighteenth Century.**

The science of musical sounds is now, with justice, considered as the art that unites corporeal with intellectual pleasure by a species of enjoyment which gratifies sense without weakening reason; and which, therefore, the great may cultivate without debasement, and the good enjoy without depravation.   Burney.

155.

June 3d.   **Music's Refining Power.**

A dull man, to whom the conceptions of the grandest master of instrumental music are incomprehensible—to whom Beethoven unlocks no portal in heaven—suddenly hears the human voice of the human singer, and at the sound of that voice the walls that enclosed him fall. He of himself, poor man, can make nothing of it. He cannot say, "I am an inch nearer to heaven," but the feeling that he *is* an inch nearer to heaven abides with him. Unconsciously, he is gentler, he is less earthly, and, in being nearer to heaven, he is stronger for earth. BULWER LYTTON.

156.
A Universal Language. June 4th.

It may be that music will become a universal language, when the majority will cease to regard that art solely as a means to tickle the ear or to set the foot in motion; when men will study musical science, and thus see analogies between great musicians and other great thinkers, between Dante and Bach, Shakespeare and Beethoven, high priests whose sublime hymns shook the intellectual world from its mediæval lethargy. Then, perhaps, instead of being thought a frivolous amusement, this language will be valued as the highest metaphysical manifestation of mankind.

LOUIS LOMBARD.

157. June 5th.

Music is the language spoken by angels.

LONGFELLOW.

158.
A Voice from the Sixteenth Century. June 6th.

Touching musical harmony, whether by instrument or by voice, it being but of high and low in sounds a proportionable disposition, such, notwithstanding, is the force thereof, and so pleasing effects it hath in that part of man which is most divine, that some have thereby been induced to think that the soul itself is or hath in it harmony; a thing which delighteth all ages, and beseemeth all states; a thing as seasonable in grief as in joy; as decent being added unto actions of the greatest weight and solemnity as being used when men most sequester themselves from action: the reason hereof is an admirable facility which music hath to express and represent to the mind, more inwardly than any other sensible means, the very steps and inflections of every way, the turns and varieties of all passion whereunto the mind is subject. HOOKER.

159.

June 7th. **Unity in Variety.**

Music may be termed the universal language of mankind, by which human feelings are made equally intelligible to all; whilst, on the other hand, it offers to the different nations the most varied dialects, according to the mode of expression suitable to the character of each nation. LISZT.

160.

June 8th. **Praise for the Piano.**

Let no one say the moral effects of music are small or insignificant. That domestic and long-suffering instrument, the piano, has probably done more to sweeten existence, and bring peace and happiness to families in general and to young women in particular, than all the homilies on the domestic virtues ever yet penned. H. R. HAWEIS.

161.

Its Spirit is Love. June 9th.

Music is the essential nature of things, and its kingdom is not of this world. Its spirit, like that of Christianity, is love, and it excites within us, as soon as we are filled with it, the highest ecstasy of the consciousness of illimitability. **WAGNER.**

162.

The Minor Key. June 10th.

As long as love continues the most imperious passion, and death the surest fact of our mingled and marvellous humanity, so long will the sweetest and truest music on earth be ever in the minor key. **ANON.**

163.

An Ideal Representation. June 11th.

It is music which discovers and explains for us the beautiful in the world and in the mind, or, still more, which shows us in the movements of the world and of the mind that inner life which a spiritual nature reveals, so that, amid the external in which we are engaged, the conditions of mind and soul may express themselves, or through sound make us acquainted with the things of their life. The representation of the ideal in a concrete form is the aim of music because music is art. The tone art shows the play of various emotions —it is an ideal representation of the individual life and of its soul-melodies. **CARRIERE.**

164.
June 12th. **Music in the Home.**

The habitual use of vocal music by a family is an almost unfailing sign of good morals and refined taste.

C. W. LANDON.

165.
June 13th. **Refine the Taste.**

Music and painting both appeal primarily to the senses, the one to the eye, the other to the ear. Hence arises a special difficulty; for who shall decide what is really true and beautiful when this is, after all, only a question of taste? Let us ever bear in mind what Schumann says, when he insists on the necessity for a thorough knowledge of the form, in order to attain a clear comprehension of the spirit. So will our taste become refined and pure, our instinct true and unerring; enabling us to choose the good and reject unhesitatingly the false and meretricious.

RIDLEY PRENTICE.

June 14th. ### 166.

I verily think, and am not ashamed to say, that, next to Divinity, no art is comparable to music.

MARTIN LUTHER.

167.
June 15th. **Sentiment and Science.**

Music is at once a sentiment and a science; it demands of him who cultivates it, be he executant or composer, natural inspiration and a knowledge which is only to be acquired by protracted studies and profound meditations. The union of knowledge and inspiration constitutes art. Outside of these conditions the musician will be nothing more than an incomplete artist, if, indeed, he deserve the name of artist at all.

BERLIOZ.

168. June 16th.

Music is the only one of all the arts that does not corrupt the mind. MONTESQUIEU.

169.

Music Extending Its Sway. June 17th.

Music, it is well to remember, is playing well its important part. Grave or gay, it is penetrating everywhere: making itself an essential part of every religious, educational, or social function. It is beautifying the playtime of the child, and making of its study a pleasure; it adds its refining influence to fashionable affairs, giving them a dignity they did not always possess; it is recognized as a superior means of relief from inane gossip, as a means of diversion which, when set forth by artists, gives more than it promises and leaves no bitter taste in the mouth.

Addison declared that music is the only sensual gratification which mankind may indulge in to excess without injury to their moral or religious feelings. However true this may be, it is certain that music is the one most important element in social recreation to-day, and that the constantly increasing interest shown in it is one of the strongest indications of a tendency to good morals and to consequent good manners. ANON.

170.

June 18th.   **Each His Own Measure.**

Every person has a lead with which he attempts to measure the depths of art. The string of some is long, that of others is very short; yet each thinks he has reached the bottom, while in reality art is as a bottomless deep that none have as yet fully explored, and probably none ever will. Art is endless.

SCHOPENHAUER.

171.

June 19th.   **All Deep Things are Song.**

All deep things are song. It seems somehow the very central essence of us, song; as if all the rest were but wrappages and hulls! The primal element of us; of us, and of all things. The Greeks fabled of Sphere-Harmonies: it was the feeling they had of the inner structure of nature; that the soul of all her voices and utterances was perfect music. See deep enough, and you see musically; the heart of nature *being* everywhere music, if you can only reach it.

CARLYLE.

172.

June 20th.   **God's Best Gift.**

Music is God's best gift to man, the only art of heaven given to earth, the only art of earth we take to heaven. LANDON.

June 21st.   173.

I cannot conceive of the spirit of music otherwise than in love. WAGNER.

174.
The Heart the Interpreter. June 22d.

Music has many mysteries, many, indeed, that will never be explained. Its very motives and tributaries are mysterious; for no man understands the secrets of his own heart, the language of his own soul. The heart is inspired by so many sentiments that we seek in vain for the key to their consequences. The soul is a thing religiously spiritual, and from the infiniteness of its motives the results are incomprehensible. Yet we can ascertain the incentives which give operation to the soul, and the objects which cause emotion to the heart. Music seems to be the only language that can perfectly express those innate and internal emotions. The immediate effect—the spontaneous sensation, is communicated from heart to heart; and these being the expression of some inward, effervescent passion, the mind cannot explain them; the heart must be their only interpreter. A. J. GOODRICH.

175.
True of the Enthusiast. June 23d.

The art of music is hardly one for a dreamer. It is an exacting art, and one which admits of only the most industrious form of leisure, to use a paradox. The idle moments of a musician are so few that they may be very easily counted. ANON.

176.
Morals. June 24th.

Not only health but morals are promoted by the cultivation of music. It is not only a safeguard against sickly and unwholesome habits, as I have shown, but against immoral ones. Refined pleasures, like music, stand in the way of grosser tastes.

W. C. BRYANT.

177.

June 25th. **A Common Origin.**

If we turn back to the path of development in speech and music and cast an eye on its origin, it then appears that they have the same source in common. Both were identical in primeval times. Music was speech, speech was music; for early in primeval times, when speech was forming, speech must have been music, inasmuch as both have a common essence as a foundation. By the primeval word emotions were aroused and brought to expression, just as this is the essence of music. The primeval word differed from the word of the present day in this way, that then it was a sign of emotion, now it is a sign of knowing. HERMANN RITTER.

178.

June 26th. **Not Second to Intellect.**

In its bearing upon human happiness we believe that the emotional language which musical culture develops and refines is only second in importance to the language of the intellect; perhaps not even second to it! HERBERT SPENCER.

179.

June 27th. **A Poetical Medium of Expression.**

Music is the art which applies sounds—the sounds that result from periodical vibration and have definite pitch, as distinguished from casual noises—to the presentation of imaginative figures or clearly arranged ideas. It is the poetical medium of expression for what is not in the province of literature, of sculpture, of acting, or of architecture. Whereas, literature, whether in prose or verse, describes or states emotions, or perceptions, or impressions; whereas, sculpture imitates the outward forms of animated beings, and physiognomy either in the face of, or, to speak more broadly, in the moulding and attitude of the entire figure, displays personal character, and the effect of passion upon it; whereas, painting vitalizes with color the forms of sculpture, and extends its range of subjects from animate to inanimate nature; and, whereas, acting adds speech to the written words of the dramatist, enforcing or even qualifying their meaning by vocal inflection, and illustrating it by changeful gesture, thus giving the mobility of life to the forms of sculpture and painting, music embodies the inward feelings of which all other arts can but exhibit the effect. WALTER MACFARREN.

180.
A Classic View. June 28th.

Music, that perfect model of elegance and precision, was not given to men by the immortal gods with the sole view of delighting and pleasing their senses, but rather for appeasing the troubles of their souls and the sensations of discomfort which imperfect bodies must necessarily undergo. PLATO.

181.
Solace in Music. June 29th.

When an audience disperses, can you guess what griefs the singer may have comforted, what hard hearts he may have softened, and what high thoughts he may have awakened?   BULWER LYTTON.

182.

June 30th.   **Echoes from Above.**

The glorious bursts of harmony that thrilled and quivered through the brain of Händel, the pealing triumphs of the Hallelujah Chorus, the glowing reveries of Mozart, the gorgeous sonatas of Beethoven, the tender melodies of Mendelssohn, and all the exquisite conceptions of the most gifted masters, may be only faint and far-off echoes to the grander performances above; yet, as echoes, they bring down something of heavenly music to the conceptions of men on earth, and make us yearn and bend before the thought, "If these be *echoes*, what must the realities be?

ANON.

July 1st. ### 183.

A musical composition is a poem. Read it. Let it touch your soul with heavenly fire.   E. E. AYRES.

184.

July 2d.   **The Beginnings of Music.**

Music is no less an element in nature than light, air, electricity, or the heat of the sun. It is manifest in the thunder, in the sighing winds of the forest, in the surge of the ocean, in the cry of the beasts of the field, in the song of the birds of the air. Its human manifestation began with the first song of primeval man and the moan of the first infant, accompanied by the twitter of the first bird and by the bleating of the first lamb on the slopes of the Asiatic mountains.

Music as a practical art is as old as humanity itself. It is prehistoric. Its beginnings are lost in the myths and mysteries of history, and will never be known until the origin of races, tribes, and nations are discovered by the searching ethnologist. Nor has there yet been found a tribe among men that does not possess something of music in its nature and practice it, either by voice or instrument, however discordant this music may seem to the cultivated ear. W. FRANCIS GATES.

185.
To Discipline Emotion. July 3d.

The future mission of music for the millions is the discipline of emotion. What is the ruin of art? *Ill-regulated emotion.* What is the ruin of life? Again, *ill-regulated emotion.* What mars happiness? What destroys manliness? What sullies womanhood? What checks enterprise? What spoils success? constantly the same—*ill-regulated emotion.* HAWEIS.

186. July 4th.

Music speaks the most universal of languages, one by means of which the soul is freely yet vaguely inspired. SCHUMANN.

187.
How Many Realize it ? July 5th.

Music is life, spiritual life. When the teacher and pupil realize this fact a world of beauty heretofore undreamed of will reveal itself to them. They will have an incentive to work, which will cause them to perseveringly overcome all necessary mechanical requirements of technic and notation, and will enjoy their work as those cannot do who have lower aims and less noble views of their art.   Anon.

188.
July 6th.   **To the Heart.**

Music has a higher mission than merely to please the ear. It is the art which appeals most powerfully to the heart, and through this affects character.

    Merz.

189.
July 7th.   **A Natural Means of Expression.**

The art of tone has this advantage over the arts of painting and sculpture, viz., that music is a natural and universal means of expression. There can never be symphonies of color, as has been imagined, for the reason that nowhere in the world is color naturally (as distinguished from artistically) employed to express anything. Tone, on the contrary, is universally so employed. When the birds sing, or the child cries, or the dog barks, we have the beginning of music, for it is the beginning of the use of tones to express feeling. Ordinary speech expresses, not ideas alone, but also feeling. The voices rise and fall, the intervals and the time change, increasing and diminishing as the feeling changes. Whenever speech ceases to convey merely cold intellectual ideas, and becomes emotional, the voice tends more and more toward a song, ranging more widely through the gamut and taking on the cadences of music proper. Even among the elements of speech we have the beginnings of music, the vowels themselves being pure tones. E. R. SILL.

190.
Music in Speech. July 8th.

Observe how all passionate language does of itself become musical—with a finer music than the mere accent; the speech of a man even in jealous anger becomes a chant—a song. All deep things are song.
THOS. CARLYLE.

191.
Farther than Speech. July 9th.

Music begins where speech leaves off; through it the inmost spirit—all that is inexpressible and yet of most account in us—can give itself. Hence the loftiest poetry, the most inspired and subtle charm of conversation, in short, that magical something which distinguishes the utterance of genius in its high hour, in whatsoever form, is analogous to music and sets the fine chords vibrating in somewhat the same manner.
DWIGHT.

192.
Added Force. July 10th.

Although music is in its nature indefinite, it is capable of being attached to definite ideas, and of giving them a force and intensity obtainable by no other means.
WILLIAM BELLARS.

193.
Art Growth. July 11th.

Music is never stationary; successive forms and styles are only like so many resting places—like tents

pitched and taken down again on the road to the ideal.
FRANZ LISZT.

194.

July 12th.   **Teach Your Children Music.**

You will stare at a strange notion of mine; if it appears even a mad one, do not wonder. Had I children, my utmost endeavors should be to make them musicians. Considering I have no ear, nor even thought of music, the preference seems odd, and yet it is embraced on frequent recollection. In short, as my aim would be to make them happy, I think it the most probable method. It is a resource which will last them their lives, unless they grow deaf; it depends upon themselves, not on others; always amuses and soothes, if not consoles, and of all fashionable pleasures is the cheapest. It is capable of fame without danger of criticism, is susceptible of enthusiasm without being priest-ridden; and, unlike other mortal passions, is sure of being gratified in heaven.
HORACE WALPOLE.

195.

July 13th.   **Highly Specialized Art.**

Music is a highly specialized form of art; perhaps, on the whole, the most highly specialized art that we have. It is specialized in two directions—an inner soul-life of great sensitiveness, and an outer manifestation through highly complicated combinations of sounds, which in turn appeal to the soul through the hearing apparatus, which must be very sensitive and discerning. The higher forms of music are forever reserved

for these two classes of hearers—those of great sensitiveness and imaginative power of soul, and those who have, along with this musical type of soul, a hearing apparatus of corresponding nobility and discernment.
W. S. B. MATHEWS.

196.
Rhythm and Beauty.   July 14th.

Art has as its fundamental law, the law of beauty. Beauty presupposes symmetry. Symmetry is visible rhythm. Rhythm is audible symmetry or symmetrical motion. Symmetrical motion is the ground-element of music. CHRISTIANI.

197.
The View of a Lawmaker.   July 15th.

Of all the liberal arts, music has the greatest influence over the emotions, and is that art to which the lawmaker should give great attention.
NAPOLEON BONAPARTE.

198.
The Art of the Prophets.   July 16th.

Music is the art of the prophets, the only art that can calm the agitation of the soul; it is one of the most magnificent and delightful presents God has given us.
LUTHER.

199.   July 17th.

Music was taught to Achilles in order to moderate his passions. HOMER.

200.

July 18th.   **Music Makes Character.**

Has it ever occurred to you that musical practice has the power to form and perfect the character of the faithful student? On the piano, or any other instrument, you soon discover that you must be *conscientious* in the matter of every detail or you will not succeed. That is one good quality to acquire and cultivate, which will give you a good name and make you morally strong. You will also become convinced that you must be patient and persevering, or else, figuratively speaking, the barrel which you are making such an effort to roll up hill will roll down hill, and you will have to begin again. Patience and perseverance are great virtues to possess—the first indispensable to the teacher, the second a *sine qua non* to those who would become finished performers. I might go on enumerating other excellences of character which musical practice makes grow within us, but the hints given will suffice.

Robert Goldbeck.

201.

July 19th.   **A Means of Culture.**

Music is a means of culture; it is one of the greatest and, perhaps, the greatest factor in human civilization. Not until men shall use the art with a spirit of reverence will it exercise those powers for which it is designed. The present generation of philosophers and teachers are only beginning to search for the real meaning and explanation of the art, and they have not advanced sufficiently to answer even these simple questions: What is music? Wherein consists its great power? KARL MERZ.

202. July 20th.

The question of music for the people will some day become a great government question.

H. R. HAWEIS.

203.
The Object of Music. July 21st.

It is the exclusive object of music to express feelings and affections. The extension and development of the power of expression in music consists in the capacity for describing special affections, and this capacity for describing special affections it acquires only by being blended with speech. SCHUMANN.

204.
With Sweet Emotion. July 22d.

My idea is that music ought to move the heart with sweet emotion, which a pianist will never effect by mere scrambling, thundering, and arpeggios—at least not from me. BACH.

205.
The Musical Brain. July 23d.

Let me remind you of a curious fact with reference to the seat of musical sense. Far down below the great masses of thinking marrow and its secondary agents, just as the brain is about to merge into the spinal cord, the roots of the nerve of hearing spread their white filaments out into the sentient matter, where they report what the external organs of hearing tell them.

This sentient matter is in remote connection only with

the mental organs, far more remote than the centres of the sense of vision and that of smell. In a word, the musical faculty might be said to have *a little brain of its own*. It has a special world and a private language all to itself. How can one explain its significance to those whose musical faculties are in a rudimentary state of development or who have never had them trained? Can you describe in intelligible language the smell of a rose compared with that of a violet? No; music can be translated only by music. Just so far as it suggests worded thought, it falls short of its highest office. Pure emotional movements of the spiritual nature— that is what I ask of music. Music will be the universal language—the Volapuk of spiritual being.

Dr. O. W. HOLMES.

206.

July 24th.   **A Natural Medium.**

Music is the natural medium of emotional expression; feelings that stifle utterance, too strong to be conveyed in simple words, are breathed melodiously to the hearts of men in the universal language of music.

AUSTIN.

207.

July 25th.   **The Pure Art.**

Did you ever consider that music is the one art that is absolutely pure? The sculptor may so shape his clay or his marble statue that it shall suggest evil thoughts. The artist may put upon the canvas the bacchanalian drinking-scene, and bring all the degradation of human life before you and into your imagination. Even the architect, with the aid of subsidiary arts of decoration, may contrive rather to injure than to uplift mankind. But music never can be made by itself a means or a voice of degradation. You may mate it to words that are degrading, and so drag it down. You may cluster about it degrading associations, and so drag it down. But the voice of music itself cannot be so perverted as to be other than a voice pure and clean and sweet. LYMAN ABBOTT.

208.
Not to be Contaminated. July 26th.

All beauty is essentially holy and can be polluted only externally by contact with meaner things; but, on account of its immateriality, music is less liable to permanent contamination than the other arts.
JAMES C. MOFFAT.

209.
Mistress of Order. July 27th.

The youth must always be accustomed to this art, for it makes good and virtuous citizens. Music is a discipline, a mistress of order and good manners. She makes the people milder and gentler, more moral, and more reasonable. MARTIN LUTHER.

210.
A Memory Cultivation. July 28th.

No study so strengthens and enlarges the memorizing power as does music. It is a continual memory cultivation, and the results of close application to musical memorization approach the bounds of the incredible. In witness of this we may cite the feats of Mozart, Liszt, Bulow, Rubinstein and others. A number of pianists have been able to produce by memory all of the Bach fugues and Beethoven sonatas. Many compositions played in a proper *tempo* require the production of over a thousand tones per minute.

A certain blind flutist could play any one of one hundred and twenty-five concertos called for by number. Many an operatic star has a repertoire of a score of operas. The great conductors like Nikisch and Seidl know the Beethoven symphonies and the Wagnerian dramas practically by heart, and conduct them without score. And this is largely the result of the study of music. What it has done for these masters of music it may do in some degree for us, in proportion to our natural abilities. W. F. GATES.

211.

July 29th. **Upon Our Heart Strings.**

Music is to our hearts as is the wind to the Æolian harp. It plays upon our heart-strings; and while we hear the sound of the strings, and imagine that it is the instrument that vibrates, it is our own hearts which in reality vibrate; our hearts are bleeding while the instrument is but dead wood. MERZ.

212.

July 30th. **An Inclusive View.**

Music is an art; the highest and noblest of all arts; the art out of which all the other arts spring. Music is the basis of all the arts, the consummation of all human endeavor, the dome under which all these arts come to be what they ought to be, the inspiring atmosphere which makes all of these expressions of the human soul a definite outflow of human love toward God and toward humanity. The religion that is dearest to us finds its most beautiful inspiration in music, and its best and grandest life is gained from music.

M. L. BARTLETT.

213.
A Divine Calling. July 31st.

What a divine calling is music! Though everything else may appear shallow and repulsive, even the smallest task in music is so absorbing, and carries us so far away from town, country, earth, and all worldly things, that it is truly a blessed gift of God. MENDELSSOHN.

214.
A Woman's View. Aug. 1st.

Music is not a science any more than poetry is. It is a sublime instinct, like genius of all kinds. OUIDA.

215.
Sound Expresses Feeling; Words, Ideas. Aug. 2d.

Sounds articulate and inarticulate are among the most efficient means of expressing and conveying feeling. . . . Thus, anger, hatred, joy, love, jealousy, eager expectation, desire, passionate remorse, gentle regret, sadness, or melancholy are conveyed unmistakably by sounds, whether connected with words or not. Let it be noticed that words, the signs of ideas, only excite feelings *indirectly* by conveying ideas which raise the feelings; while sounds convey these feelings *directly* and immediately. It is by the natural extension and carrying out of this process that the sounds produced by instruments have come to be associated with the same feelings which the voice expresses by tones in speech and song, so that music has come to be a highly complex and elaborate *language of emotion*—a perfect medium for the expression of feeling.

JOHN C. FILLMORE.

216.
Aug. 3d. **In Spite of Abuse.**

If, in spite of all the abuse and ill-treatment to which it is subjected, the noble art of music never ceases to charm and edify us, it only attests its unfathomable and everlasting grandeur. FERDINAND HILLER.

217.
Aug. 4th. **Incompatible Traits.**

I think that I can answer for it that if a man loves music he generally loves charity. I have found very few men who love gardening and were drunken—very few men who love song and were churlish.

GEORGE DAWSON.

218.
Aug. 5th. **Awakening the Better Nature.**

Music is not only a passing, sensual pleasure; it often awakens emotions of a deeply spiritual character, which reveal to the individual a truer knowledge of the better nature within him than he himself has ever before realized. In listening to such music he suddenly finds himself rising to a plane of thought and feeling which is far removed from any he has ever before experienced. His material outer self, which hitherto dominated all his thoughts and actions, gives way to a realization of the nobler soul that dwells within but has been lying dormant until the kiss of music awakened it from sleep. FRANK DAMROSCH.

219.
Straight to the Heart. Aug. 6th.

There is something very wonderful in music. Words are wonderful; but music is even more wonderful. It speaks not to our thoughts as words do—it speaks straight to our hearts and spirits, to the very core and root of our souls. REV. CHAS. KINGSLEY.

220. August 7th.

A song will outlive all sermons in the memory.
H. GILES.

221.
Music Covers the Whole Emotional Gamut. Aug. 8th.

Music exists for the expression of varied emotion—sadness, longing, hope, triumph, aspirations toward the unobtained or the indefinite, calm fulfilment of an artist's conception of fitness and beauty; and, besides these, monotony, long spell of unbroken quiescence, mental perturbation even to a positive sense of physical discomfort, are absolutely essential to relieve and heighten the more ecstatic emotions of pleasure called forth by a musical composition. We cannot always be burning with passion and reciting dramatic duets or heading triumphal processions. We do not do so in real life. It is not only vivid impressions that are interesting; these heaped up, one upon another, constitute a plethora of over-strained excitement that will jade and exhaust the most passionate nature. There are countless experiences in life which leave us in a tranquil condition of enjoyment; and, since these make up far the greater portion of our existence, and are the vehicle of the most powerful emotions, are they not worthy of a prominent place in so comprehensive an index of human sentiment as is music? CHAMBERS.

222.

Aug. 9th. **A Novelist's Musical Nature.**

As to myself, however, I love everything musical, the lively music as well as the sad and classical, the music of Beethoven, the music of the Spaniards, Glück and Chopin, Massenet and Saint-Saens, Gounod's "Faust" and "Marionette," the folk-songs, the hand-organ, the tambourine, even the bells, music for dancing and music for dreaming. It all speaks to me, inspires me. Wagner's music moves me, thrills me, hypnotizes me, and the violin harmonies of the gypsies, those sorcerers of music, have always drawn me to the exhibition. The despicable fellows always stop my progress. I cannot leave them. ALPHONSE DAUDET.

223.

Aug. 10th. **For the Masses.**

Music is designed for the masses, it belongs to the masses, it is one of the principal means, outside of Christianity, to refine the masses. MERZ.

224.

Aug. 11th. **Grand Music.**

Grand music is the utterance of emotions for which language is too slow, too cold, and too confined.
G. D. HAUGHTON.

225.
An Element of Culture. Aug. 12th.

Music is an important element of modern culture, a refining social influence, a subject about which few cultivated persons nowadays are willing to be thought ignorant or indifferent, an art which in one way or another, actually interests more thousands of people, more occupies their thoughts, more ministers to their enjoyment, than any science, or than most branches of literature and learning.   DWIGHT.

226.
A Plea for Early Cultivation. Aug. 13th.

Music, more, perhaps, than anything else on earth, affords a sweet foretaste of those ecstatic joys which, we are fain to hope, are to be hereafter.

So universal is music in its influence and sway, that its extinction—were this possible—would leave a blank and a chasm almost as vast, as dreadful, as desolating, and as overpowering as the extinction of the very sun itself.

If legislators were wise they would so frame laws that every child should have a thorough and systematic course of musical instruction whilst at school, since there is nothing at present known which is better calculated than music, especially vocal music, to transform children into good fathers, good mothers, good citizens, and good Christians in the best sense of this much-abused and misunderstood word.

All properly constituted human beings possess the faculty to produce and the power to enjoy music, of some kind or other, and the only reason why the vast majority of them do not turn this faculty and this power to proper account is, that they do not sufficiently cultivate and train them. JOHN POWERS.

227.
Aug. 14th. **The Greatest Art.**

Sometimes we speculate whether music is not doomed to be the next, the chiefest, and perhaps the greatest, manifestation of art of which mankind is capable.

GEORGE DAWSON.

228.
Aug. 15th. **Concrete and Abstract Musicians.**

Music is a language; it should be taught and studied as such; we listen to it, hear it, think it, speak or interpret it, read it, and write it. Musicians at large, be they composers, teachers, interpreters, or *litterateurs*, are divisible into two classes, namely, those who understand the language and those who do not. The work and expression of the former are sincere, ardent, and spontaneous; of the latter, mechanical and labored. The former may be called concrete musicians, the latter abstract musicians. JULIUS KLAUSER.

229.
Aug. 16th. **Better Some Music Than No Music.**

The science of music, as well as painting and drawing, contains often in later years fountains of genuine pleasure for those even who have but a limited knowledge of art. Therefore it should never be asserted that music exists exculsively for the talented; on the contrary, let every lover of music prosecute this study, but let it be in a practical manner.   Kohler.

230.   Aug. 17th.

Music does not cover a little excited bit of life, but the whole of life.   Edmund Gurney.

231.

Echoes from Heaven.   Aug. 18th.

Is it possible that that inexhaustible evolution and disposition of notes, so rich yet so simple, so intricate yet so regulated, so various yet so majestic, should be a mere sound which is gone and perishes? Can it be that those mysterious stirrings of heart, and keen emotions, and strange yearnings after we know not what, and awful impressions from we know not whence, should be wrought in us by what is unsubstantial, and comes and goes, and begins and ends in itself? It is not so, it cannot be. No; they have escaped from some higher sphere; they are the outpourings of eternal harmony in the medium of created sound; they are echoes from our home; they are the voice of angels, or the magnificat of saints, or the living laws of divine governance, or the divine attributes; something are they besides themselves, which we cannot compass, which we cannot utter.   Cardinal Newman.

232.

A Notable Saying.   Aug. 19th.

Man is so inclined to give himself up to what is common, and the sense of what is beautiful and perfect is so easily blunted in the mind and thought, that to feel and appreciate the beautiful must be by all means retained; for none can afford to dispense with such enjoyment, and it is only because men are not accustomed to the enjoyment of what is good, that so many men find pleasure in what is common and tasteless if it is but new. Every day one should at least hear a little song, read a good poem, and gaze upon a fine picture, and, if it be possible, speak a few sensible words.

Goethe.

233.
Aug. 20th. **Do Something Worthy.**

Have you real talent—real feeling for art? Then study music—do something worthy of the art—and dedicate your whole soul to the beloved saint.

Longfellow.

234.
Aug. 21st. **Communicated Feeling.**

The language of tones is at the same time a symbol, a sort of symbolic representation of feeling. It has the power to call forth the same emotions in the hearer as those by which the tone-poet was immediately affected.

H. Ritter.

235.
Aug. 22d. **A Concise Definition.**

Music is the art of moving, by a systematic combination of sounds, the affections of intelligent, receptive, and cultivated beings. Berlioz.

Aug. 23d. ### 236.

Music is a calculation which the soul makes unconsciously in secret. Leibnitz.

237.

Gladstone's Views.   Aug. 24th.

There are very few people who are wholly without musical faculty and feeling. If they are without it, it is because it has never been cultivated in them. I remember when I was young I used to dispute with people about that. They said: "It is all nonsense to talk about music as a gift to the generality of mankind. The faculty of music is only given here and there, to one man here, and one woman there, etc., and it is an extremely rare endowment." I deny that. I say if it is properly tended, and properly brought out, it is a general gift in civilized, and even in barbarous, countries; and most certainly it is a gift that pervades the people of England, so far as nature's part is concerned. But people used to say to me, "I cannot sing." I said, "Supposing that when you were a baby, and when you grew out of being a baby, your nurse always continued to carry you in her arms, do you think you would be able to walk? I am sure not. Well, you learn to walk by practising walking, and you must learn to sing by practising singing." Beyond singing lies instrumental music, and there the progress made has been astonishing. It was to the last degree rare when I was young; it has now become very common.

WM. E. GLADSTONE.

238.

Its Purpose.   Aug. 25th.

Melody, both vocal and instrumental, is for the raising up of men's hearts and the sweetening their affections toward God.   HOOKER.

239.

Aug. 26th.   **Finer Than Speech.**

The meaning of music lies hidden in those deep mysterious changes of everyday experience which it were as vain to ignore as it is impossible to render into words. Music is finer than speech and makes its appeal to a deeper somewhat in us underlying all thought of the understanding. Music expresses that part of our best and utmost consciousness, which needs such sympathetic fluid, one might almost say electric language, as its tones alone afford.   DWIGHT.

240.

Aug. 27th.   **A Partial Knowledge.**

Music, if only listened to and not scientifically cultivated, gives too much play to the feelings and fancy; the difficulties of the art draw forth the whole energies of the soul.   J. P. RICHTER.

241.

Aug. 28th.   **Crystallized Sound.**

Music is the crystallization of sound There is something in the effect of a harmonious voice upon the disposition of its neighborhood analogous to the law of crystals.   H. M. THOREAU.

Aug. 29th.   ### 242.

Music is God's voice reflected by Nature into man's consciousness.   ANON.

243.

Aug. 30th.   **Preaches Universal Brotherhood.**

Man everywhere, in all ages, naturally manifests his feeling in song. He does not instinctively express himself in sculpture and painting, and hence those arts appeal only to the cultivated few. But music is the universal language; it needs no interpreter; when a man hears it he recognizes his mother-speech, and it is the tenderest and truest part of him that makes reply.

Music, therefore, declares that mankind is a unit; it preaches universal brotherhood. The occasions on which music is employed and its relation to social habits and observances are the same everywhere. The interests that have the most moving influence upon men in their collective capacity are those of religion and patriotism, and music acts as the most powerful intensifier of the ardor with which these two ideas inspire the soul. If love of music should die out, patriotism would lose half its enthusiasm, and the spirit of worship would feel that it had lost its best interpreter. All the functions of social life are everywhere idealized by the art of song. Among many nations every form of industry has its special song, for thus is toil lightened and unity of effort insured. EDW. DICKINSON.

244. Aug. 31st.

Music belongs to no country, and we value beautiful music from whatever part of the globe it may come.
C. M. VON WEBER.

245.

Modern as an Art. Sept. 1st.

Music is the most modern of all arts; it commenced as the simple exponent of joy and sorrow (major or minor). The ill-educated man can scarcely believe that it possesses the power of expressing particular passions, and therefore it is difficult for him to comprehend the more individual masters, such as Beethoven and Schubert. We have learned to express the finer shades of feeling by penetrating more deeply into the mysteries of harmony. ANON.

246.
Sept. 2d. **A Poetic Fancy.**

Music, rather than poetry, should be called "the happy art." She imparts to children nothing but heaven, for as yet they have not lost it, and lay no memories as mufflers on the dear sounds. J. P. RICHTER.

247.
Sept. 3d. **Theory as a Foundation.**

Music is a language more potent than any other, and the greatest fault lies in ignorance of home influence just on this point. How many parents realize that if their children be musical and apt the one great essential is the rigor of rightness? Music is such a developer, such a sanitary adjunct to life, such an educator, that all there is in a true musician's life is the perfection of his or her art. If you can get mothers to believe that theory lessons, three times a week for twenty minutes at a time, at home or in some first-class conservatory, is the only foundation for musical excellence, you have placed the first brick in that household for the musical corner-stone. ANON.

248.
Sept. 4th. **What Music Requires of Us.**

Music, the art, is based on music, the science. It is founded on rhythm, which is essentially mathematical.

A close study of acoustics and tonal relationships

requires considerable mathematical research. An analysis of the structure of instruments reveals the mathematical science as their basis. In the study of applied music the performer must continually use the calculative faculties with a rapidity and precision that astounds the novice.

No art or science requires more alertness, more accuracy, more concentration of thought and action than the proper performance of the master works. Added to this, there is continually exercised the executant's powers of discrimination in the matters of tone-color, shading, and *nuance*. He must grasp the most complex harmonies; he must interpret the most elusive points of emotional expression.

Musical theory in its various subdivisions—acoustics, harmony, composition, orchestration, etc., is, as a mental gymnastic, the equal of any study of college or university; to this the student of musical theory will promptly bear witness. And being as taxing to the mental powers, it is, as a consequence, equally valuable as an intellectual factor. But while music, thoroughly studied, is the equal of other branches of learning in its powers of mind development, it should by no means be substituted for a general curriculum. Art without science and literature is as incomplete as are literature and science without art.   W. FRANCIS GATES.

249.
There are Also Weeds.   Sept. 5th.

Musical art recognizes two kinds of music—artistic music, the production of the artist, and national music, the production of the people. If we liken music to flowers the former would be the cultivated, the latter the wild flowers. CHRISTIANI.

250.

Sept. 6th. **The Outcome of Character.**

Music, to be worthy of serious regard, must stand as the outcome of its composer's character, and primarily of his original imaginative power. If the work be really part of a man's self, it will reproduce his features, it will speak with his voice. HADOW.

251.

Sept. 7th. **At Lowest Ebb.**

Music is at its lowest ebb when taken as a mere pastime for the senses. The flood is reached when it is suggestive of noble thoughts and fancies.

A. W. BORST.

Sept. 8th. ### 252.

Sweet melodies are those which are by distance made more sweet. WORDSWORTH.

253.

Sept. 9th. **The Essence of Music.**

The essence of music may be described as the far dark currents of the soul, the fleeting life, the constant whirl of the world into which all existence and all repose are drawn; as all that rises, hovers, and trembles in the air, and in the heart of man, all that the soul re-echoes to itself from the varied phenomena of movement. KRUGER.

254.

Music Not the Cause of Failure.   Sept. 10th.

Our sensibilities and emotions make up by far the greater part of life; and among all the arts and sciences none has so great effect and influence upon them as music. We therefore contend that if a man amounts to nothing outside of music, the lack of mental ability is not due to the art of music in itself, but to the man as originally endowed; just as in any special study a man who devotes his time and attention to that alone will, in all probability, not be a success outside of his special field of work, nor necessarily in it. But who would think of claiming that the study in itself was to blame, when the man had neglected all others?

E. A. SMITH.

255.

A Part of Our Existence.   Sept. 11th.

No art is exercising such a strong influence over the human race at the present time as the art of music. It has become so thoroughly a part of our existence that we rarely pause to consider to what an extent we are, as it were, enveloped in its sweet sounds, or how irremediable its loss would be to us.

JOHN STAINER.

256.

A Statesman and Warrior.   Sept. 12th.

I love music above all the arts, especially Beethoven's. Home music is my greatest delight. I have always been sorry that I was obliged in my student days to omit music from my course. That was a misfortune, for, like all Germans, I am tuned by nature in harmony with music. BISMARCK.

Sept. 13th. 257.

Music is the atmosphere of the soul and of the senses set in motion simultaneously. ANON.

258.

Sept. 14th. **Sense, Intellect, and Emotion.**

The action of music is threefold—upon the senses, upon the intellect, and upon the emotion. All these faculties must be refined, strengthened, and directed to their proper objects, if the right impression of music is to be received. And I hold that music itself, correctly studied, tends to develop the healthy powers of the perception, the intelligence, and the feeling, and thus co-operates with other liberal studies in achieving the great purpose of education. EDW. DICKINSON.

259.

Sept. 15th. **Rhythmic Architecture.**

Music is *architecture* translated or transposed from space into time; for in music, besides the deepest feeling, there reigns also a rigorous, mathematical intelligence. HEGEL.

260.

Sept. 16th. **To Make Men Content.**

The man who can play the piano sufficiently well, and whose musical education enables him to read at sight, can find enjoyment in life, however depressing his outward circumstances may be. After a day's uncongenial work he can sit down to his piano and forget everything, himself, his poverty, the meanness and petty sordidness of many of the natures with which he has been brought into contact during the day, and commune with the spirits of great men, and feel that, for the moment, he is of the same clay as they. That, to my mind, should be the aim of education: to make men content with their lot, reliant on themselves for their enjoyment in life; to make them see the beauty there is in existence if one looks but a bare inch below the surface; to develop their human instincts so that in their relations with the world they shall show a human sympathy which is absent in those who are ever seeking to make something out of their fellow-men, and at their expense. ANON.

261.
Pure Art. Sept. 17th.

Music is undoubtedly the purest of all arts; all the others are liable to the intrusion of some prosaic elements. Music alone presents always the characteristics of pure poetry. WILLIAM BELLARS.

262.
Recreation for Mind and Body. Sept. 18th.

That which I have found the best recreation both to my mind and body, whensoever either of them stands in need of it, is music, which exercises at once both body and soul, especially when I play myself; for then, methinks, the same motion that my hands make upon the instrument, the instrument makes upon my heart.
J. BEVERIDGE.

263.
Sept. 19th. **An Inherent Power.**

Music alone has the inherent power of interpreting transcendent affections with absolute truth. In power of expression it leaves the sister arts far behind it.

FRANZ.

264.
Sept. 20th. **The Speech of Angels.**

Music is well said to be the speech of angels; in fact, nothing among the utterances allowed to man is felt to be so divine. It brings us near to the Infinite; we look for moments, across the cloudy elements, into the eternal Sea of Light, when song leads and inspires us. Serious nations, all nations that can listen to the mandate of nature, have prized song and music as the highest—as a vehicle for worship, for prophecy, and for whatsoever in them was divine. CARLYLE.

265.
Sept. 21st. **Music's Uses.**

Music is useful for strengthening our mental energy and ideas, refreshing our imagination, reviving our sensitiveness and relieving our fatigue. H. CHOMET.

266.
Sept. 22d. **A Narrower View.**

Music, the art of moving intelligent men, gifted with special and practised organs, by combination of tones. To thus define music, is to admit that we do not believe it to be, as people say, *made for everybody*. Whatever may be the conditions of its existence, whatever may have been its means of action at any time, whether simple or complex, mild or energetic, it has always been evident to the impartial observer that, as a great number of persons cannot either feel or comprehend its power, those persons *were not made for it*, and consequently, it was not made for them. BERLIOZ.

267.
Creation's Harmonies. Sept. 23d.

Music is the harmonious voice of creation, an echo of the invisible world, one note of the divine concord which the entire universe is destined one day to sound.
MAZZINI.

268.
To Young People. Sept. 24th.

In music especially, you will soon find what personal benefit there is in being serviceable; it is probable that, however limited your powers, you have voice and ear enough to sustain a note of moderate compass in a concerted piece—that, then, is the first thing to make sure you can do.

Get your voice disciplined and clear, and think only of accuracy, never of effect or expression. If you have any soul worth expressing, it will show itself in your singing; but most likely there are very few feelings in you at present needing any particular expression, and the one thing you have to do is to make a clear-voiced little instrument of yourself, which other people can entirely depend upon for the note wanted.
JOHN RUSKIN.

269.

Sept. 25th. **What Music in Heaven?**

Lord, what music hast Thou provided for Thy saints in heaven, when Thou affordest bad men such music on earth? ISAAK WALTON.

Sept. 26th. ### 270.

Experience teaches that music does not remain at such places where the devil rules.

MICHAEL PRAETORIUS.

271.

Sept. 27th. **Music Never Corrupt.**

Music is the highest of the arts. The musical artist is nearest to being a creator. The architect must study the woods and mountain caves as models of the structure he would erect; the painter copies the scenes of nature; the poet gets from life the experience which he puts into beautiful language; the musician alone is never an imitator, certainly never when at his best. Though he may suggest the thunder and the rain, the call of the bird, or the roar of battle, the music that lives—that makes one willing to say with Paul that "he knows not whether he is in the body or out of the body"—such music is never imitative. As Browning has it: the musician out of three sounds makes, not a fourth, but a star. Other arts may be corrupt; music is never corrupt, even though associated with corrupt words. LYMAN ABBOTT.

272.

Sept. 28th. **Music Should be Pleasing.**

Passion, whether great or not, must never be expressed in an exaggerated manner; and music—even in the most harrowing moment—ought never to offend the ear, but should always remain music, which desires to give pleasure. MOZART.

273. Sept. 29th.

Music is a pleasing accomplishment; let the fair learn to sing. OVID.

274.
Music Is Suggestive. Sept. 30th.

The beauty of truth is fundamental to art. The term art implies that the beauty of certain truths is concealed, hence it is the mission of art to suggest, to reveal, and perpetuate the beauty of truth. The office of the artist is to entice the beauty of truth from its concealment and present it, not only so persuasively that its self, the truth, and its beauty are revealed, but so delicately that one sees neither the art nor the artist, only the truth.

Music is the highest form of art, because her mode of revelation is suggestive rather than structural or delineative. ANON.

275.
Superiority of Vocal Music. Oct. 1st.

I am sure if anything on earth can give an idea of the angelic choir, it must be the music of Palestrina. And yet I do not forget the glorious effect of Handel; but all music to which instruments contribute must be a degree more earthly than that in which human voices are alone to themselves sufficient, where nothing mechanical is needed. BARONESS BUNSEN.

276.

Oct. 2d. **Music is Non-material.**

The worth of art appears most earnest in music, since it requires no *material* or *subject matter*, whose effect must be deducted; it is wholly form and power, and saves and ennobles whatever it expresses.

GOETHE.

277.

Oct. 3d. **Seek Good Music, Not Bad.**

It has long been a question for discussion as to whether music has done more harm than good in the world, which, after all, resolves itself into an individual one: Has it done *me* more harm than good? There is no doubt that many people read a class of books having only a pernicious influence—but this is not the fault of literature; people select these books from choice, and the individual alone is responsible. So it is with music. There are certain associations and influences at work that are demoralizing, and they draw largely upon music for their attractiveness; but one need not seek these. They are not obliged to listen to the trashy, or encourage the taste for such music, unless it be their own wish. Because a few who may be members of the church do wrong, does not imply that religion or the church is to blame? Neither is the great art of music; such responsibility must rest upon the individual.

E. A. SMITH.

Oct. 4th. #### 278.

Music is the revelation of the inmost dream-image of the essential nature of the world.

WAGNER.

279.
Familiarity Breeds Greater Delight.   Oct. 5th.

The effect of good music is not caused by its novelty. On the contrary, it strikes us more the more we are familiar with it.   GOETHE.

280.
Music Associated With Sense Perception.   Oct. 6th.

It is one of the limitations of music that it holds no relation to reason. Music is entirely outside the sphere of reason. The latter begins to act only when it is furnished with distinctly formulated conceptions, or thoughts, and these are not found in music. Reason and music, therefore, have nothing in common with each other, but belong to different departments of the soul. Music goes in with sense perception, and addresses the feelings directly as such. It can give us a prolonged action of the soul, an emotional history, and in this is its great superiority in spirituality to other forms of art. The proper sphere of music is to portray the progress of the soul from grief or sadness to comfort, joy, and blessedness. This it can do with an intelligibility entirely its own. Whatever is bright, tender, joyful, daring, noble, music expresses with peculiar force. It is the art of the ideal sphere of the soul, the sphere into which sin and its consequent sufferings have never entered. Evil is outside of its pure providence.   HEGEL.

281.
Music in the Public Schools.   Oct. 7th.

The moral and æsthetic influence of music is admitted on all hands, and a knowledge of its elements at least is of great value in the formation of a correct musical taste. Our interest in life is not wholly centred in material pursuits. Our natures are highly complex, and should be expanded and cultivated in various directions, and especially in whatever tends toward elevation and refinement. The public school should lay the foundation of morals, and music is clearly recognized as one of the moral forces by all students of sociology. HAWLEY.

282.

Oct. 8th. **Who, then, Gets to the End?**

Ye pedlers in art, do ye not sink into the earth when ye are reminded of the words of Beethoven on his dying bed, " I believe I am yet but at the beginning "?
SCHUMANN.

Oct. 9th. ### 283.

We have learned to express the finer shades of feeling by penetrating more deeply into the mysteries of harmony. SCHUMANN.

284.

Oct. 10th. **The Expression of the Immaterial.**

To the inapt or uncultured, music seems but the graceful or forcible union of sounds with words, or a pleasant, meaningless vibration of sound alone. But to him who has read the open secret aright, it is a language beyond all others for the expression of the soul's life. The true musician cares very little for your definite ideas, or things which can be expressed by words —he knows you can give him these; what he sighs for is the expression of the immaterial, the impalpable, the great imponderables of our nature, and he turns from a world of painted forms and oppressive substances to find the vague and yet perfect rapture of his dreams in the wild, invisible beauty of his divine mistress.

HAWEIS.

285.
Music's Refining Tone.   Oct. 11th.

I regard music not only as an art whose object it is to please the ear, but as one of the most powerful means of opening our hearts and of moving our affections.

GLUCK.

286.   Oct. 12th.

Music is love; it springs from religion and leads to religion.

HANSLICK.

287.
The Joyous Art.   Oct. 13th.

It may be an unphilosophic fancy of mine, which a stern logician would demolish, but to my mind there is a beautiful significance in the fact that music, this universal art, to which men have always confided the most sacred experiences of their souls, is almost invariably an art of joy. Its pervading tone is one of happiness. It is not so with the other arts. The student of the world's poetry is struck by the undertone of sadness that runs through it—his contact with its greatest minds leaves him, on the whole, depressed. Painting and sculpture have depicted the pain almost as often as the pleasure of human life. But it is the glow and rapture of existence of which the world's music speaks. Not that music has no sympathy with sorrow, but when she enters into scenes of mourning she does so not to make more vivid the poignancy of grief, but rather to console. EDW. DICKINSON.

288.
Oct. 14th. **Inarticulate Speech.**

The meaning of song goes deep. Who is there that in logical words can express the effect that music has on us? A kind of inarticulate, unfathomable speech, which leads us to the edge of the infinite and lets us for a moment gaze into that. CARLYLE.

289.
Oct. 15th. **No Sweeter Voice.**

Among the instrumentalities of love and peace, surely there can be no sweeter, softer, more effective voice than that of gentle, peace-breathing music.

ELIHU BURRITT.

290.
Oct. 16th. **Is Music Aristocratic?**

Chopin's frequently quoted remark to the effect that music is essentially an aristocratic art, only serves to show how nonsense will pass for wisdom, if only it has some great name to back it. Music! why it is the only one of the arts that ever makes its home among the lowly; that takes even the street Arab out of the filth, ignorance, and degradation which he knows too well, to give his soul an occasional glimpse of the sunshine, an occasional breath of the pure air of song-land. Music is not essentially aristocratic; it is universal, therefore essentially democratic, Chopin to the contrary notwithstanding. ANON.

291.
Abstract Training. Oct. 17th.

As the study of geometry trains the mind in the abstract, so the study of music trains the emotions in the abstract. ANON.

292.
The Governor of the Heart. Oct. 18th.

According to the Holy word of God, nothing deserveth to be so highly praised and extolled as music, and for this reason, that music is the strong and mighty governor of every movement of the human heart (to say naught of the hearts of beasts at present) by which man is often governed and overcome, even as it were by a master.

Nothing on earth is stronger, to make the sad joyful, the joyful sad, and the timid bold, to charm the haughty to humility, to calm and quiet hot and excessive love, to lessen envy and hatred, and if any one can recount to me all the emotions of the human heart by which people are swayed, and driven either to virtue or vice, I will say, that nothing is more mighty than music to curb and govern these same emotions of the mind.

MARTIN LUTHER.

293.
Effective Music. Oct. 19th.

The popular mind, when left to itself, has a natural sympathy for music that truly and healthily reflects the genuine emotions of mankind; and there is no more effectual way of working upon it than by music of an elevating kind. THIBAUT.

294.
Oct. 20th. **Materia Musica.**

Music finds an infinitely rich but totally amorphous and plastic material in musical tones, which may be shaped into form, unfettered by any of the restrictions that apply to other of the fine arts. Painting and sculpture, for instance, are fettered by the necessity for imitating nature; poetry must conform to the existing symbolical meaning of sounds; architecture must consult utility of construction; but music is absolutely free to dispose of her material in any way whatever which the artist may deem most suitable for his purpose.   HELMHOLTZ.

295.
Oct. 21st. **Genius in Music.**

Where there is genius, it does not much matter in what manner it appears—whether in the depth, as in Bach, or in the height, as in Mozart, or whether alike in depth and in height, as in Beethoven.

SCHUMANN.

Oct. 22d. ### 296.

Music is the greatest painter of soul-conditions, and the worst of all for material objects.   AMBROS.

297.
Oct. 23d. **Music the Language of the Emotions.**

A very little reflection will show us that music is not necessarily connected with any definite conception. Emotion, not thought, is the sphere of music; and emotion quite as often precedes as follows thought. Athough a thought will often, perhaps always, produce an emotion of some kind, it requires a distinct effort of the mind to fit an emotion with its appropriate thought. Emotion is the atmosphere in which thought is steeped —that which lends to thought its tone or temperature —that to which thought is often indebted for half its power. H. R. HAWEIS.

298.
Threefold Benefit. Oct. 24th.

The benefit which I wish my pupils to derive from tuition is threefold—to heart, ear, and hands; they are as it were the root, blossom, and fruit of tuition.

SCHUMANN.

299.
Music Not a Trifle. Oct. 25th.

They who think music ranks amongst the trifles of existence are in gross error; because from the beginning of the world down to the present time it has been one of the most forcible instruments both for training, for arousing, and for governing the mind of man. There was a time when letters and civilization had but begun to dawn upon the world. In that day music was not unknown; on the contrary, it was so far from being a mere servant and handmaid of common and light amusement that the great art of poetry was essentially wedded to that of music, so that there was no poet who was not a musician; there was no verse spoken in the early ages of the world but that music was adapted as its vehicle, showing thereby the universal consciousness that in that way the straightest and most effectual road would be found to the heart and affections of men.

WILLIAM E. GLADSTONE.

300.

Oct. 26th.   **Folk Music of Antiquity.**

The musical art is a great fact. It is older than Christianity, older than Mohammedanism; it was old when the soldiers of Cæsar landed on the shores of Great Britain; old when Alexander carried the civilization of Asia to Europe. It antedates Rome and Athens and the years of Confucius and Buddha, David and Solomon; and our brothers of the long ago may have sung at the foundations of the pyramids of Egypt.

Dr. Thomas.

301.

Oct. 27th.   **Live In It.**

To the true artist music should be a necessity and not merely an occupation; he should not manufacture music, he should live in it.   Robert Franz.

302.

Oct. 28th.   **The Voice the Living Instrument.**

We have already said that, if possible, everyone should learn music; we now pronounce our opinion more specially, that "everyone, if possible, should learn singing." Song is man's own true peculiar music. The voice is our own peculiar connate instrument. It is much more; it is "the living sympathetic organ of our souls." Whatever moves within us, whatever sensation or emotion we feel, becomes immediately embodied and perceptible in our voice; and so, indeed, the voice and song, as we may observe in the earliest infancy, are our first poetry and the most faithful companions of our feelings.

If, as in song properly so-called, music and speech be lovingly united, and the words be those of a true poet, then is consummated the most intimate union of mind and soul, of understanding and feeling—that combined unity in which the whole power of the human being is exhibited, and exerts upon the singer and the hearer that wonderful might of song which by infant nations was considered, not quite untruly, as supernatural. BERNHARD MARX.

303.
Artistic Ramifications. Oct. 29th.

When we come to regard the art of music in its broader outlines, we find that its relationship with things immediately outside of music is indeed very intimate. Art education in any branch is a compound; it is something which, like bread, is made from some one material, to which are added in small quantity, though in an exact proportion, certain other ingredients, and all these form an *ensemble*, pleasing to the taste and nourishing to the whole system.

THOS. TAPPER.

304.
The Eternity of Music. Oct. 30th.

Music was the first sound heard in the creation, when the morning stars sang together. It was the first sound heard at the birth of Christ, when the angels sang together above the plains of Bethlehem. It is the universal language, which appeals to the universal heart of mankind. It greets our entrance into this world, and solemnizes our departure. Its thrill pervades all nature—in the hum of the tiniest insect, in the tops of the wind-smitten pines, in the solemn diapason of the ocean. And there must come a time when it will be the only suggestion left of our human nature and the creation, since it alone, of all things on earth, is known in Heaven. The human soul and music are alone eternal. GEORGE P. UPTON.

Oct. 31st. 305.

Such sweet compulsion doth in music lie.

MILTON.

306.

Nov. 1st. **An Intense Pleasure.**

It is a pity that it is impossible to acquire musical culture as easily as reading and writing; for the pleasure of diving into the depths and beauties of the score of a masterwork is as great and intense a pleasure as any in the whole range of art. ROBERT SCHUMANN.

307.

Nov. 2d. **A Philosopher's Musings.**

Music surpasses every other of the imaginative arts in exciting enthusiasm; in winding up to a high pitch those feelings of an elevated kind which are already in the character, but to which this excitement gives a glow and a fervor, which, though transitory at its utmost height, is precious for sustaining them at other times.

This effect of music I had often experienced, but like all my pleasurable susceptibilities it was suspended during the gloomy period; I had sought relief again and again from this quarter, but found none. After the tide had turned, and I was in process of recovery, I had been helped forward by music, but in a much less elevated manner. I this time first became acquainted with Weber's "Oberon," and the extreme pleasure which I drew from its delicious melodies did me good by showing me a source of pleasure to which I was as susceptible as ever.

The good, however, was much impaired by the thought that the pleasure of music (as is quite true of such pleasure as this was, that of mere tune) fades with familiarity, and requires either to be revived by intermittence or fed by continual novelty. And it is very characteristic of my then state of mind, that I was seriously tormented by the thought of the exhaustibility of musical combinations. The octave consists only of five tones and two semi-tones, which can be put together in only a limited number of ways, of which but a small proportion are beautiful. Most of these, it seemed to me, must have been already discovered, and there could not be room for a long succession of Mozarts and Webers to strike out, as these had done, entirely new and surpassingly rich veins of musical beauty. This source of anxiety may, perhaps, be thought to resemble that of the philosophers of Laputa, who feared lest the sun should be burnt out. JOHN STUART MILL.

308.
No Corrupt Music. Nov. 3d.

Music may be applied to licentious poetry, but the poetry then corrupts the music, not the music the poetry. It has often regulated the movement of the lascivious dances, but such airs, heard for the first time, without the song or dance, could convey no impure idea to an innocent imagination, so that Montesquieu's assertion is still in force that "Music is the only one of all arts which cannot corrupt the mind."

DR. BURNEY.

309.

Nov. 4th.   **An Unpleasant Truth.**

The great mass of the population does not yet know the elevating effect of real music. How can it be possible with our present mode of music-education, which has been made a lucrative field for private speculation, to find out that the creations of Bach, Mozart, Beethoven, Listz, and Wagner are more important and of deeper concern than all the shallow and transitory creations of salon composers, who just live (in regard to musical power of reproduction) on the incapability of the public? It is not surprising that the great works of Richard Wagner found no echo in the public in early years.   HERMANN RITTER.

Nov. 5th.   310.

To hear superior music played in a superior way is an education.   THOMAS TAPPER.

311.

Nov. 6th.   **Our Music is a Modern Art.**

What we call *music* is a new art, in the sense that it very probably bears little resemblance to what the civilized peoples of antiquity called by that name. Besides, we must say at once, that word had such an extended acceptation with them, that, far from signifying simply the art of tones, as it does to-day, it applied equally to dancing, pantomime, poetry, eloquence, and even to all the sciences together. Supposing that the etymology of the word *music* is contained in *muse*, the widely extended meaning the ancients gave it is naturally explained; it meant and must have meant, *that over which the muses preside.* BERLIOZ.

312.
Music Needed in America. Nov. 7th.

In America, more than anywhere else, is music needed as a tonic, to cure the infectious and ridiculous business fever which is responsible for so many cases of premature collapse. HENRY T. FINCK.

313.
Study Music as Literature. Nov. 8th.

If music is worth studying at all, it is as literature, poetry, an expression of the beautiful, and as product of some of the most gifted minds who have expressed themselves for the delectation of their fellow-men. Music has in it a poetry and a beauty, and a many-sided representation of soul, far beyond that of literature. The poetry of the piano-forte is more varied and more spiritually representative than that of the English language. But the point is, *how* is the student to be brought into contact with this poetry, when his study of music is, after all, only an accomplishment and a diversion among his earnest occupations? Obviously, I answer, in the same manner as similar results are attained in the literary schools—by so coördinating the studies that the student, while supposedly working for the immediate lesson, is also working along a longer line toward this lofty and distant goal of culture.

W. S. B. MATHEWS.

314.

Nov. 9th. **Music is Independent.**

Music excites emotion independently of all foreign aid. Words and gestures add nothing to its power; they only enlighten the mind in regard to the object of its expression. FETIS.

315.

Nov. 10th. **No Denominationalism in Music.**

Music is the humanest of all the arts—it brings men together. Organists or members of church music-committees may doubt the statement by reason of some experiences; but nevertheless it is true that music is a great unifier. There is no schism, no heresy, no denominationalism, in music. Music stirs to worship, and whatever stirs to worship is orthodox; there is no heretical music. The church may question the source of its doctrines, but it takes its hymns from all sources —Roman Catholic, Protestant, Calvinistic, Arminian, Evangelical, and Unitarian. Music has this unifying power beyond creed or preaching, because it expresses the profoundest experiences and sentiments of the human heart; sentiments which nothing else can express. Music is the most sacred of the forms of expression because it goes deepest and gives voice to those feelings common to humanity; hence it is that music has the highest place in the sanctuary.

LYMAN ABBOTT.

316.

Nov. 11th. **The Misuse of Music.**

I despise all superficial, frivolous music, and never occupy myself with it. The object of music is to strengthen and ennoble the soul. If it does else save honor God and illustrate the thoughts and feelings of great men, it entirely misses its aim. But what shall I say of those men who, gifted with the divine power of creating music, misuse their power in a contemptible manner? There are such men, however, on whose ingratitude it is impossible to look without indignation. And their works alone are those that deserve the epithets, enervating, demoralizing. But, should anyone pretend to say that *all music* is a frivolous luxury, he may rest assured that the frivolity and other defects besides are to be looked for *in his own breast* and not in the nature of music.   MORALES. [About 1510.]

317.

A Beautiful Expression.   Nov. 12th.

A distinguished philosopher spoke of architecture as *frozen* music, and his assertion caused many to shake their heads. We believe this really beautiful idea could not be better reintroduced than by calling architecture "*silent*" music.   GOETHE.

318.

Words Do Not Explain Music.   Nov. 13th.

Music is more definite than words, and to seek to explain its meaning in words is really to obscure it. There is so much talk about music, and yet so little really said. For my part, I believe that words do not suffice for such a purpose, and if I found that they did suffice, then I certainly would compose no more music. People often complain that music is so ambiguous that what they are to think about it always seems so doubtful, whereas overyone understands words. With me it is exactly the reverse, not merely with regard to entire sentences, but also to individual words. These, too, seem to be so ambiguous, so vague, so unintelligible, when compared with genuine music, which fills the soul with a thousand things better than words. What any music I love expresses to me is not thought too indefinite to be put into words, but, on the contrary, too definite. MENDELSSOHN.

319.
Nov. 14th. **Always Appropriate.**

Music is a strangely peculiar form of the beautiful, whose presence seems, indeed is, appropriate on occasions the most diverse in character. Its aid is sought alike to add to the joys of festive scenes, to soothe and elevate the heart on occasions of mourning, and to enhance the solemnity, the excellence, of divine worship.
TROTTER.

320.
Nov. 15th. **Life is Music.**

All one's life is music, if one touches the notes rightly, and in time. RUSKIN.

321.
Nov. 16th. **The Power of Indefiniteness.**

The art which expresses itself merely through variations of pitch and accent is undoubtedly too vague, too indefinite, to be universally understood. However, in this very indefiniteness lies its power. All the other arts and languages seek to define, to limit, to end; while music—unfathomable mystery!—expands beyond the horizons. Words describe emotions, perceptions, impressions; sculpture and architecture imitate the forms human eyes have seen; painting vitalizes such forms with earthly colors; acting, through vocal inflections and mobile gestures, endeavors to portray our innermost feelings; but music does all this and much more. From the indefinite realm of the mind it evolves an imagery surpassing the pictorial and the plastic arts; with words that paint, it tells every passion; and in grandeur and solemnity it overshadows even the temples of Babylon. That which is too vast and beautiful to be displayed before man, the gods suggest through music. LOUIS LOMBARD.

322.
The Divinity of Music. Nov. 17th.

The divinity of music is only perceived when it lifts us into an ideal condition of existence; and the composer who does not do this much, is, as far as we are concerned, a mere hewer of wood and drawer of water.
THIBAUT.

323.
Musical Study Productive of True Culture. Nov. 18th.

To speak of the pervading intellectuality of the masterworks of music would open up a field of indefinite scope. It must be enough for us to recognize, in but a passing way, this element as a dominant feature of the works of Bach, Beethoven, Brahms, Schumann, Berlioz, Wagner, and their co-laborers. Music has its Shakespeare, its Milton, its Tennyson, its Longfellow, and the intellectuality of the artist in music is not less marked than that of the artist in poetry.

The study of the masterworks in music is as productive of mental culture as equivalent application to the study of general literature or science; a different kind of culture, to be sure, but not the less real culture, for all that. Culture, refinement, is something more than a storing away of facts, calculations, and theories. It is an appreciation of fine distinctions, of high ideals, of lofty conceptions—a development of the finer powers of mind and heart as well as of the stronger and coarser faculties. Nothing in science so successfully reaches this side of our natures as does the study of art, and nothing in art more gently or thoroughly than music.

W. Francis Gates.

324.

Nov. 19th. **Music the Gift of God.**

Often have I said from my very soul with Luther—and will here say again—" Music is a fair and glorious gift of God. I would not for the world forego my humble share of it."

Thibaut.

325.

Nov. 20th. **The Earthly Grammar of Heaven's Language.**

Music is a language which, properly understood and correctly expressed, gives voice to those loftier and sweeter emotions of the heart and mind which common language is powerless to convey. Prose expresses the prose thoughts and ideas of existence; poetry advances a step and translates feelings, pleasures, and passions beyond the province of prose; and music advances yet another step, and becomes the medium for those evanescent, dream-like imaginings which dwell in a region beyond the dense atmosphere which surrounds this work-a-day world. " In Heaven they speak in music!" yet the instructed eye and the sympathetic soul may read these dream-glimpses on the printed page, may learn the laws which govern their modes of expression, and, finally, may translate them in sound to other souls. Though music be the language of Heaven, its grammar is taught on earth. R. S. HANNA.

326.
A Foretaste of Another World. Nov. 21st.

Music moves us, and we know not why; we feel the tears, and cannot trace the source. Is it the language of some other state born of its memory? For what can wake the soul's strong instinct of another world like music? LETITIA LANDON.

327.
Full of Truth and Beauty. Nov. 22d.

Music is a rich field that needs the best it can receive. Whoever will seek broad education in and out of music, whoever will endeavor to keep in hand some of the common threads of tendency that join music and the development of thought, whoever will seek with care and patience the use and place of art in daily life, will discover that music offers them no little as a beautiful inheritance, no little as a sacred trust. It is full of unexplored ways; they should be made known to us. It is full of truth; we should constantly know more of it. It is full of beauty; we should see it all. It is a world full of thought and inspiration; we should be taught not to lose our way in it. Not less lovingly than the little child whispers to its mother should they speak of it, their own beautiful *mater sanctissima*.

THOS. TAPPER.

Nov. 23d. 328.

Music alone can take the world as she finds it, and make daily advances in popular favor.

EDMUND GURNEY.

329.

Nov. 24th. **Singing Praises With the Understanding.**

Lord, my voice by nature is harsh and untunable, and it is vain to lavish my art to better it. Can my singing of psalms be pleasing to thy ears which is unpleasing to my own? Yet, though I cannot chant with the nightingale or chirp with the blackbird, I had rather chatter with the swallow—yea, rather croak with the raven, than be altogether silent. Hadst thou given me a better voice I would have praised thee with a better voice. Now, what my music wants in sweetness let it have in sense, singing praises with understanding. Yea, Lord, create in me a new heart (therein to make melody), and I will be contented with my old voice until in thy due time, being admitted into the choir of Heaven, I have another, more harmonious, bestowed upon me. THOMAS FULLER.

330.

Nov. 25th. **Art Only to Those Who Appreciate It.**

Music is an art only to those who accept it as a revelation of the beautiful, the ideal, the spiritual, the divine. If to anyone it is mere sound, or a mere succession of sounds, however skilfully arranged, while it may excite the emotion of wonder, it is not art.

A long while has this musical language been waiting its development; it has been in the utmost simplicity until very recent times. After all the other fine arts had reached a high state of excellence, and had operated with many other powerful agencies of Christian civilization in educating the sensibilities of men, and in lifting men upward to a higher plane of spiritual existence—then Music came to claim her place. ANON.

331.
Happy People. Nov. 26th.

All musical people seem to be happy. It is the engrossing pursuit—almost the only innocent and unpunished passion. SIDNEY SMITH.

332.
The Power of Music. Nov. 27th.

Music is not a mere mechanical quality; it is an element of the soul. Wagner has aptly described it as "the inarticulate speech of the heart, which cannot be compressed into words, because it is infinite." It is the language of feeling. While words cannot fully express it, yet they are the best vehicle we have for the utterance thereof. Music, therefore, when combined with words, has its greatest power. Music illuminates feeling, and appropriate words illuminate music. Carlyle, with a keen musical insight, observes that "all inmost things are melodious, and naturally utter themselves in song. The meaning of song goes deep. Who is there that in logical words can express the effect music has on us? A kind of inarticulate, unfathomable speech which leads us to the edge of the Infinite, and lets us for a moment gaze into that." Dr. M. R. Drury.

333.
Nov. 28th. **Woman's Song.**

All the elements which woman has in her nature—love, pathos, passion, poetry, and religion—combine to perfect her song and give fitting expression to the ideas of the masters. Woman's song is the first sound the child hears. May we not fancy that when the child has grown to old age, it is still the song of woman which, though inaudible to those standing around, kindles a smile upon the dying face, and brings a look of recognition to the eyes, as if they beheld once more the old familiar face of the mother, and heard the familiar voice which sung to the old man when all his world was contained in the hollow of a cradle?

George P. Upton.

334.
Nov. 29th. **All Phases of Passion.**

All phases of passion find a ready utterance in music, from the highest joy to the deepest desolation. Among emotions of tenderness are the benevolent affections, such as sympathy and the like, but this class of feelings border more on the intellectual. They represent emotion already passing into thought, and therefore were not capable of being so fully expressed by music, which in such instances requires the help of words. When words and music are happily combined there is absolutely no feeling or state of mind which cannot be reproduced by them with probably greater vitality and completeness than the original idea itself.

ARCHDEACON SINCLAIR.

335.
The Mission of the Musician. Nov. 30th.

This is our mission in life: to cause good music to be heard in the land. And it is the mission of music to lighten toil, to comfort sorrow, to sweeten the lot of all mankind. It should be our constant endeavor so to live and so to work that the heart of the world may be strengthened and moved upon by a power refining and ennobling—the power of good music. JEFFERS.

336.
Quickening the Mind. Dec. 1st.

Music is a stimulus to the intellect. This does not mean that all wonders open to us under its inspiration, for to many minds the noble thoughts of the masters which find expression in their works will always remain unknown. Minds are quickened according to their capacities, but somewhere within the ample range of musical expression there is a power able to move even the dullest mind. The effort to follow the development of the musical theme, its recognition from time to time, as it presents itself in new combinations or changes its form; the comparison of different harmonies, the thought necessary in properly discriminating the good and the bad, all stimulate the mind and enlarge its powers. R. W. HILL.

337. Dec. 2d.

Music has something holy; unlike the other arts, it cannot paint anything but what is good. RICHTER.

140   IN PRAISE OF MUSIC.

338.
Dec. 3d.　　　　　　Full of Religion.

Music is full of religion. The first tidings that ever came from Heaven to man came in music on the plains of Bethlehem.　　　　　　GEORGE P. UPTON.

339.
Dec. 4th.　　Music in the Service of Religion.

Music, dancing, poetry, architecture, sculpture, and painting originated in the service of religion. The earliest canticle recorded in holy writ was sung after the passage of the Red Sea by Moses and the children of Israel, accompanied by the women dancing; temples were afterward erected for worship, adorned with images and embellished with color.　　　　ELLA.

340.
Dec. 5th.　　　　Music in Child Education.

Of all the arts none can sway the passions and control the emotions like music. It has a subtle and pervading power over the heart and the imagination. Childhood is led by the emotions; in youth these are tempered and partially controlled by the intellect. Let music, then, take its rightful place in our schools and in all educational advancement of youth.

EMILY WAKEFIELD.

341.
Dec. 6th.　　　　　Conditioned on Love.

Of all the arts music is practised most and thought about the least. Why this should be the case may be explained on several grounds. A sweet mystery enshrouds the nature of music. Its material part is subtle and elusive. To master it on its technical side alone costs a vast expenditure of time, patience, and industry. But since it is, in one manifestation or another, the most popular of the arts, and one the enjoyment of which is conditioned in a peculiar degree on love, it remains passing strange that the indifference touching its nature and elements, and the characters of the phenomena which produce it or are produced by it, is so general. H. E. KREHBIEL.

342.
Music Humanizing and Social. Dec. 7th.

Music, perhaps more than any other art, spontaneously sets the hearer's imagination in sympathetic cooperation. Music appeals with emphatic power to the whole being of the cultivated auditor; in fact, from the first to the last note of a composition it sways and controls the hearer's emotional nature and, through this, his intellectual one also.

Music is eminently humanizing and social; it softens and neutralizes the materialistic aims of our time; it keeps up a thread of ideality between man's mind and soul. It beautifully ministers to man's existence, brings refreshing balm to his weary mind, and, for the time being, causes him to forget, while dwelling in an ideal world based on harmony and order, the depressing, inevitable worries of the everyday struggle.

FREDERIC LOUIS RITTER.

343. Dec. 8th.

Music is a life and a world in itself.

M. B. EDWARDS.

344.

Dec. 9th.   **Musical Genius.**

It is strange that nearly all the world's greatest men have grown out of poverty, and in no case is this more true than in the lives of great musicians. Genius seems like some plant that cannot flourish upon a rich soil, but matures to beauty and perfection in the bleakest air and when it is least cared for.

FREDERICK CROWEST.

345.

Dec. 10th.   **The Lasting Pleasure of Music.**

Of all the arts, music, in its acquirement and practice in domestic life, exercises the greatest influence over the social habits of our lives and frequently promotes the lasting friendship of virtuous and congenial natures.   J. ELLA.

346.

Dec. 11th.   **Music Next to Theology.**

I have always loved music, and I would not give away for a great deal the little that I know. I am not at my ease with those who have a contempt for music. Music is like a discipline—it makes men sweeter, more virtuous, and wiser. One can be sure of finding the germs of a goodly number of virtues in the hearts of those who love music, but those who have no taste for it I value as I value a stick or stone. I contend, and I declare it without shame, that after theology there is no art comparable to music. When natural music is perfected by art, we see as far as we are able, the great and perfect wisdom of God in His fine work of music. MARTIN LUTHER.

347.
Music the Breath of Germany. Dec. 12th.

Music is the Word of Germany. The German people, so much curbed as a nation, so emancipated as thinkers, sing with a sombre delight. To sing seems a deliverance from bondage. (Music expresses that which cannot be said, and which cannot be suppressed.) There fore is Germany all music, in anticipation of the time when she shall be all freedom.

Song is for Germany a breathing: it is by singing that she respires and conspires. The music-note being the syllable of a kind of undefined universal language, Germany's grand communication with the human race is made through harmony—an admirable prelude to unity. It is by the clouds that the rains which fertilize the earth ascend from the sea; it is by music that ideas emanate from Germany to take possession of the minds of men. Therefore we may say that Germany's greatest poets are her musicians, of which wonderful family Beethoven is the head. VICTOR HUGO.

348.
Music a Reflection of Its Epoch. Dec. 13th.

Music not only reflects the individuality and spiritual emotion of the composer, but is also the echo or refrain of the age, the historical events, the state of society, culture, etc., in which it was written. I am convinced that this is so even to the smallest detail of the fashion of the time in which the composer writes.

ANTON RUBINSTEIN.

349.

Dec. 14th. **Abstract Emotions.**

Music has no articulate speech. For that reason it is compelled to express emotions in the abstract. The composer can say to you, "I am sad," and in saying it he can influence you to be sad with him. But he cannot say to you in music, "I am sad because my brother is dead." The materials of musical expression do not admit of such definite statement. Music can speak a sadness more intense than words can utter, but it is the privilege of the poet, not of the musician, to tell the cause of the sadness. Music is an art which expresses moods, and it expresses them with definiteness, tremendous eloquence, and overwhelming influence.

W. J. HENDERSON.

350.

Dec. 15th. **The Dual Nature of Music.**

Music is dual in its nature; it is material as well as spiritual. Its material side we apprehend through the sense of hearing, and comprehend through the intellect; its spiritual side reaches us through the fancy (or imagination, be it music of the highest class) and the emotional part of us. If the scope and capacity of the art and the evolutionary processes which its history discloses are to be understood, it is essential that this quality be kept in view.

There is something so potent and elemental in the appeal which music makes that it is possible to derive pleasure from even an unwilling hearing, or a hearing unaccompanied by an effort at analysis; but real appreciation of its beauty, which means recognition of the qualities which put it in the realm of art, is conditioned upon intelligent hearing. The higher the intelligence, the keener will be the enjoyment, if the former be directed to the spiritual as well as to the material.

HENRY E. KREHBIEL.

351.   Dec. 16th.

It is Nature who forces us to break forth into singing when our heart is moved by great and sudden emotion—in the wail of grief, in the exaltation of joy, in the sigh of melancholy longing.   CICERO.

352.
Exterior Influences Affect Music.   Dec. 17th.

Music has followed the other arts, and taken color from the influences that moulded them. It had its day of arid classicism, such as affected literature, drama, painting, and architecture in the seventeenth century; although the grandest of pure music, that of John Sebastian Bach, was a product of that period. It afterward passed through a time of affectation and artifice that leaves its trace in Italian opera, and was favorably affected by the romanticism of this century. It shows no parity with present-day realism; but it is touched with the discontent, the self-examining spirit, of these later years not by its inclining to realism, but by its restlessness, its alternating heroism and weakness, its reckless joy and heavy gloom, its lack of cheer and settled character.   CHARLES M. SKINNER.

353.
To Refine Our Taste.   Dec. 18th.

Music and painting both appeal primarily to the senses, the one to the eye, the other to the ear. Hence arises a special difficulty; for who shall decide what is really true and beautiful, when this is, after all, only a question of taste? Let us ever bear in mind what Schumann says, when he insists on the necessity for a thorough knowledge of the form, in order to attain a clear comprehension of the spirit. So will our taste become refined and pure, our instinct true and unerring; enabling us to choose the good and reject unhesitatingly the false and meretricious.

RIDLEY PRENTICE.

354.

Dec. 19th. **No Melody, No Music.**

Melody is the golden thread, running through the maze of tones by which the ear is guided and the heart reached. Without melody music may interest, but cannot charm. Fortunately, music without melody is not conceivable. The simplest and most monotonous kind of music has melody, although its character may not be to the liking of everyone.

ADOLPH CHRISTIANI.

355.

Dec. 20th. **Sentiment Versus Sentimentalism.**

Language is pre-eminently the means of expressing our thoughts; but our thoughts should not be void of sentiment, else they are cold. Music is the language of feeling, but our sentiment should not be void of thought or else it becomes sentimentalism. Language may at times have to convey mere thought void of sentiment, but music should not convey the one without the other.

KARL MERZ.

356.
The Basis of Musical Power. Dec. 21st.

The wonderfully pleasurable feeling aroused by music is undoubtedly due to its power of suggesting and stimulating the various complex emotions.

GRANT ALLEN.

357.
Incompetent Judges. Dec. 22d.

None of the other arts is encumbered with so many prejudices as music. Though accessible to every human being, its right position in the family of arts is, in many cases, underrated; its philosophical and æsthetical meaning entirely overlooked or not understood at all. About none of the other arts has so much nonsense been written as about music. A person scarcely able to distinguish one tone or note from another, one air from another, will not hesitate to judge and condemn fine musical works in a most imperative manner; nay, I have seen criticisms, novels, and sketches on musical subjects, written by persons who could not sing or play the simplest tune, and to whom theory was a *terra incognita*.

FREDERIC L. RITTER.

358.
History in Music. Dec. 23d.

The songs of a people are the story of its life told in music. All nations have had to struggle, to fight, to build, to move, to learn the danger of war, the blessing and comfort of peace. And a nation may have the rudest story to tell that we can imagine, yet, despite that, it has a history which its wise men relate either in story or in song; but whether they have the story or not, they surely have the song.   THOMAS TAPPER.

359.

Dec. 24th. **A Musical Fancy.**

Music came upon my heart like the calm beauty of death; fancy caught the sound, and faith mounted on it to the skies. It filled the valley like a mist, and still poured out its endless chant, and still it swells upon the ear, and wraps me in a golden trance, drowning the noisy tumult of the world.   HAZLITT.

360.

Dec. 25th. **Fanatics and Devils.**

There is but one class of men who condemn music, and those are fanatics; and there is only one order of beings, according to Luther, who *hate* it, and those are devils.   MOWER.

361.

Dec. 26th. **A Modern Art.**

Music is the most modern of all arts; it commenced as the simple exponent of joy and sorrow (major and minor). The ill-educated man can scarcely believe that it possesses the power of expressing particular passions, and therefore it is difficult for him to comprehend the more individual masters, such as Beethoven and Schubert. We have learned to express the finer shades of feeling by penetrating more deeply into the mysteries of harmony.   ROBERT SCHUMANN.

362.

Music and other Arts.   Dec. 27th.

Three results follow from the distinction between music and the representative arts. First, that musical criticism is pre-eminently difficult to express with clearness and certainty. Secondly, music is of all arts the most nearly universal in its appeal. Thirdly, no law of musical science is to be taken as final.

W. H. HADOW.

363.

Music an Intellectual Product.   Dec. 28th.

Music is wholly the creation of the human intellect. It has no model in nature as painting and sculpture have. The very materials of music are the products of man's thought. Because beauty is conceived only by man, and music is the pure product of his intellect, it seems to me that this art comes nearer to an expression of beauty in the abstract than any other. It is the highest product of the imagination, and hence closer to free beauty than any other art. It proceeds out of the elements of our tripartite nature—sensation, reason, and emotion, in their most uncircumscribed and unconditioned state, and consequently it appeals to them with irresistible force.   W. J. HENDERSON.

364.

Eternal, Not Temporal.   Dec. 29th.

That which music expresses is eternal and ideal. It does not give voice to the passion, the love, the longing of this or the other individual, under these or the other circumstances; but to passion, love, longing itself.

WAGNER.

365.

Dec. 30th. **Its Ultimate Mission.**

Music is a language of feelings which may ultimately enable men to impress vividly and completely on each other the emotions they experience from moment to moment. HERBERT SPENCER.

366.

Dec. 31st. **A Long and Glorious Record.**

The long story of music is a continuous and unbroken record of human effort to extend and enhance the possibilities of effects of sound upon human sensibilities, as representing in a formal or direct manner the expression of man's inner being. The efforts resolve themselves mainly into impulses to find means to produce the effect of design, and to contrive types of expression which are capable of being adapted to such designs. And as the difficulty of coping with two things at once is considerable, men have generally concentrated their efforts on design at one time and on expression at another.

C. H. H. PARRY.

INDEX OF AUTHORS.

INDEX OF AUTHORS.

(REFERENCED TO NUMBER OF THE SELECTION.)

Abbott, J. G., 114
Abbott, Lyman, 12, 149, 207, 271, 315
Addison, Joseph, 118, 137
Allen, B. D., 24
Allen, Grant, 356
Ambros, August W., 296
Anderson, M. B., 111
Anonymous 77, 79, 83, 87, 108, 139, 140, 162, 169, 175, 182, 187' 242, 245, 247, 257, 260, 274, 290, 291, 330
Apthorp, William F., 120
Aristides, 41
Auerbach, Berthold, 131
Augustine, Saint, 10
Austin, 206
Avison, Charles, 112
Ayres, E. E., 110, 183

Bach, John Sebastian, 151, 204
Bartlett, M. L., 212
Beattie, 6
Beethoven, Ludwig von, 3, 8, 54, 100, 117
Bellars, William, 192, 261
Benbow, William, 46, 122
Berlioz, Hector, 167, 235, 266, 311
Bertini, Henri J., 148

Bevan, 116
Beveridge, J., 262
Bismarck, 256
Bonaparte, Napoleon, 197
Borst, A. W., 251
Bryant, William C., 176
Bunsen, Baroness, 275
Burney, Charles, 154, 308
Burritt, Elihu, 289
Byrd, 14

Carlyle, Thomas, 53, 171, 190, 264, 288
Carriere, 163
Chadwick, George W., 49, 124
Chambers, 221
Chateaubriand, 11
Chomet, Dr. H., 265
Christiani, Adolph F., 196, 249, 354
Church, L. R., 51, 143
Cicero, 351
Confucius, 25
Crowest, Frederic, 344

Damrosch, Frank, 60, 218
Daudet, Alphonse, 222
Dawson, George, 217, 227
De Staël, Mme., 59
Dewey, Dr., 4
Dickinson, Edward, 243, 258, 287
D'Israeli, Benjamin, 23, 33
Doerner, August, 70
Drury, Dr. M. R., 332
Dwight, John S., 9, 191, 225, 239

Eastlake, Lady, 99
Edwards, 343
Ehlert, Louis, 18

Eliot, George, 15
Ella, John, 339, 345
Elson, Louis C., 125
Emerson, Ralph W., 67
Euripides, 81

Fetis, Francis J., 138, 314
Fillmore, John C., 65, 215
Finck, Henry T., 22, 69, 312
Franz, Robert, 263, 301
Fuller, Thomas, 329

Gates, W. Francis, 63, 132, 184, 210, 248, 323
Giles, H., 220
Goethe, Johann W., 232, 276, 279, 317
Goldbeck, Robert, 200
Goodrich, A. J., 95, 174
Gladden, Washington, 86
Gladstone, William E., 237, 299
Gluck, Christopher W., 285
Gurney, Edmund, 230, 328

Hadow, W. H., 250, 362
Hall, Dr. John, 153
Halle, Sir Charles, 136
Hanna, R. S., 325
Hanslick, Edward, 286
Haughton, G. D., 224
Haweis, H. R., 135, 145, 160, 185, 202, 284, 297
Hawley, 281
Haydn, Joseph, 34, 68
Hazlitt, 359
Hegel, 45, 259, 280
Helmholz, Hermann L., 294
Henderson, W. J., 349, 363
Henry, Bertram C., 78, 94, 119, 133
Hill, R. W., 336

Hiller, Ferdinand, 27, 96, 104, 123, 152, 216
Hoffmann, 38, 92, 106
Holland, John G., 28, 88
Holmes, Dr. Oliver Wendell, 205
Homer, 199
Hooker, 158, 238
Hueffer, Francis, 98
Hugo, Victor, 32, 347

Jeffers, 335
Johnson, Samuel, 19

Kingsley, Rev. Charles, 219
Klauser, Julius, 228
Kohler, Ludwig, 229
Krehbiel, Henry E., 134, 341, 350
Kruger, 253

Landon, Charles W., 164
Landon, Letitia, 172, 326
Lanier, Sidney, 16
Leibnitz, 236
Liszt, Franz, 159, 193
Lombard, Louis, 156, 321
Longfellow, H. W., 157, 233
Lully, James, 146
Luther, Martin, 36, 74, 150, 166, 198, 209, 292, 346
Lytton, Bulwer, 144, 155, 181

Macfarran, Walter, 179
Marx, Bernhard, 302
Mason, Lowell, 48
Mathews, W. S. B., 195, 313
Mazzini, 267
Mendelssohn, Felix, 43, 147, 213, 318
Merz, Karl, 129, 141, 188, 201, 211, 223, 355
Mill, John Stuart, 307

Milton John, 305
Mirandola, 113
Moffat, James C., 208
Montesquieu, 168
Morales, 316
Mower, 360
Mozart, W. A., 272
Munger, J. J., 20

Newman, Cardinal, 231
Niecks, Friedrich, 75

Ouida, 214
Ovid, 273

Parry, C. H. H., 73, 366
Pauer, Ernst, 42
Perry, Edw. Baxter, 7, 56, 105, 115, 126
Plato, 5, 109, 180
Poe, Edgar Allan, 66
Powers, John, 226
Praetorius, Michael, 55, 80, 270
Prentice, Ridley, 71, 165, 353

Richter, John Paul, 1, 39, 240, 246, 337
Ritter, Frederic Louis, 130, 342, 357
Ritter, Herman, 31, 40, 50, 177, 234, 309
Rubinstein, Anton, 102, 348
Ruskin, John, 2, 62, 85, 93, 97, 107, 268, 320

Schopenhauer, Arthur, 30, 170
Schumann, Robert, 37, 121, 186, 203, 282, 283, 295, 298, 306, 361
Sherwood, Mrs. William, 82
Shorthouse, J. H., 44, 72, 142
Sill, E. R., 189
Skinner, Charles M., 352

Smith, E. A.; 254, 277
Smith, Sydney, 331
Sinclair, Archdeacon, 334
Spencer, Herbert, 90, 178, 365
Stainer, John, 17, 255
Sullivan, Arthur, 91

Tapper, Thomas, 303, 310, 327, 358
Thibaut, A. F., 29, 293, 322, 324
Thomas, Dr., 300
Thoreau, H. M., 241
Towers, John, 226
Trotter, J. M., 101, 319

Upton, George P., 35, 52, 57, 127, 304, 333, 338

Van Cleve, John S., 58, 64, 128

Wagner, Richard, 47, 161, 173, 278, 364
Wakefield, Emily, 340
Waller, William, 76
Walpole, Horace, 194
Walton, Isaak, 269
Weber, C. M. von, 61, 89, 244
White, Kirke, 103
Whiting, Charles G., 84
Willeby, Charles, 21
Wordsworth, William, 252
Work, Rev. E. W., 26

Zelter, Carl F., 13

www.ingramcontent.com/pod-product-compliance
Lightning Source LLC
Chambersburg PA
CBHW030302170426
43202CB00009B/849